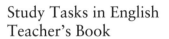

Study Tasks in English
Teacher's Book

ENGLISH FOR ACADEMIC PURPOSES titles from Cambridge

Study Skills in English *by Michael J. Wallace*

Study Listening – Understanding lectures and talks in English *by Tony Lynch*

Study Writing – A course in written English for academic and professional purposes *by Liz Hamp-Lyons and Ben Heasley*

Study Speaking – A course in spoken English for academic purposes *by Tony Lynch and Kenneth Anderson*

Study Reading – A course in reading skills for academic purposes *by Eric H. Glendinning and Beverly Holström*

Study Tasks in English *by Mary Waters and Alan Waters*

Study Tasks in English

Teacher's Book

Mary Waters
Alan Waters

Published by the Press Syndicate of the University of Cambridge
The Pitt Building, Trumpington Street, Cambridge CB2 1RP
40 West 20th Street, New York, NY 10011–4211, USA
10 Stamford Road, Oakleigh, Melbourne 3166, Australia

© Cambridge University Press 1995

First published 1995

Printed in Great Britain by

A catalogue record for this book is available from the British Library

ISBN 0 521 42614 6 Student's Book
ISBN 0 521 46908 2 Teacher's Book
ISBN 0 521 46907 4 Set of two cassettes

WD

Contents

Acknowledgements

The authors and publishers are grateful to the authors, publishers and others who have given permission for the use of copyright material. It has not been possible to trace the sources of all the material used, and in such cases the publishers would welcome information from copyright holders.

Extract 3 on p. 75 reprinted with permission from K. B. Everard and G. Morris (1985) *Effective School Management* Copyright 1985 Paul Chapman Publishing Ltd. London; extract 4 on p. 75 from 'Facing the challenge' in *EG Sourcebook* © The *Guardian* 1992; extract on pp. 76–7 from T. Radford: 'Climate' © The *Guardian* 1990; extract on pp. 77–8 from Graham Gibbs: *Teaching Students to Learn* 1981 Open University Press; extract on p. 78 from R. M. Smith: *Learning how to Learn* 1983 Open University Press; extract on pp. 82–3 from 'The perils of ignoring stress' by Dr Alistair Ostell from The Sunday Times of 31 July 1988 © Dr Alistair Ostell/Times Newspapers 1988; extract on pp. 83–4 from V. Chaudhary and Dr M. Weller: 'A history of war's killing code' © The *Guardian* 1991.

Study Tasks in English is intended to enable non-native speakers of English, of intermediate level and upwards, to acquire the skills needed for English-medium higher education study.

To use *Study Tasks in English* effectively, students should have already attained a level of at least 4.5 on the IELTS examination scale, or a score of 450 points on the TOEFL, or the equivalent.

Each unit provides between twenty to thirty hours of classroom material.

A: MAIN FEATURES OF *STUDY TASKS IN ENGLISH*

The principal features of *Study Tasks in English* are as follows:

i) A task-based approach

We believe that there is no single best way to study successfully, and that it is thus important for students to find out for themselves which study techniques suit them best. *Study Tasks in English* is therefore task-based. Whenever possible, students learn about the skills they need and how to use them through a process of discovery and induction, rather than by telling. We believe this helps the learning to be deeper and more personalised. Such an approach also helps the learner to get used to learning more independently – an essential skill in higher education.

However, we also believe it is important that the learners and the teacher should be clear about what the intended major learning points of the tasks are. We have therefore built a degree of structured guidance into the tasks, in order to try to strike a balance between the need to give learners an opportunity to think for themselves, and the need for learning outcomes to be concrete and tangible. In other words, we have attempted to sketch in the overall destination and the general direction of travel, but have left the means of travel and exact itinerary as open as possible.

ii) Study skills AND study competence

Studying can be seen as consisting of two main levels, namely a study skills level and a study competence level. The study *skills* element is made up of individual techniques of study, such as note-taking, skimming/scanning, using a bibliography and so on. The *competence* aspect is a general capacity for study, consisting of self-confidence, self-awareness, the ability to think critically and creatively, independence of mind, and so on.

Study competence is the foundation on which mastery of study skills rests. Being able to ask critical questions, for example, is an integral part of study techniques such as revising an essay draft, searching for references, examining statistical data and so on.

Thus, throughout *Study Tasks in English*, the focus is first and foremost on building up study competence. We regard a knowledge of the techniques of study as vitally important also, and this too is therefore a major focus of *Study Tasks in English*. However, in our approach, study skills are always acquired within a framework of study tasks that concentrates in the first instance on building up the underlying cognitive and affective capabilities needed for effective study.

iii) Tone

Learning to study in English can be a daunting task. *Study Tasks in English* therefore frequently includes cartoons and other types of illustrations in order to make serious points in a light-hearted way. Likewise, some of the content and activities are deliberately less academic, especially in the first few units, in order to help the student over the initial 'hump' of grasping difficult concepts and skills. At the same time, we have tried to maintain a sufficiently serious tone throughout, in order to take into account expectations of this kind as well.

iv) Analysis AND synthesis

Most of the units in *Study Tasks in English* concentrate on helping learners to acquire individual skills or sets of them. This is necessary for the sake of clarity and depth of treatment. However, the skills themselves obviously form part of a larger whole, and so it is vital to provide opportunities for learners to put the skills together into larger units as well. In *Study Tasks in English* this is done in two main ways. First, each unit in Parts A and B ends with an application activity, which gets the students actively to draw together the threads of the unit in question. Second, in Part C (*Study practice*), students work through four major study simulations, each of which is designed to consolidate and give further practice, through an integrated study cycle, in the skills studied in other parts of the book.

v) Awareness-building

We believe that it is very important to encourage study skills students to take as much responsibility as possible for their learning. Many of the tasks in *Study Tasks in English* thus take the form of review and reflection activities. Each unit of *Study Tasks in English* ends with a major self-assessment task, to help the learners actively reflect on their level of mastery of the skills which they have focused on in the unit as a whole. There is also a *Study Skills Profile* chart (in Part D), which can be used to help the teacher and the students keep track of and evaluate the students' progress at any point throughout the book.

vi) Use of English

Study Tasks in English provides numerous opportunities for learners to use their English. Although the main purpose of each of the tasks is to help the students to learn how to study, they also involve a great deal of valuable practice in all of the four main language skills. This is because the tasks require the learners to think, to make decisions, to exchange information, to be creative and so on. Thus, working through *Study Tasks in English* should improve not only the students' ability to study, but their ability to use English as well.

However, *Study Tasks in English* is not primarily an English language teaching book. For students who also need to improve their basic knowledge of English vocabulary, grammar, pronunciation etc., we would recommend using *Study Tasks in English* alongside appropriate ELT materials.

B: OVERVIEW OF CONTENTS

Study Tasks in English is divided into four main Parts:

Part A: General skills (Units 1–3)
These units foster self-awareness about learning and the thinking and questioning skills needed for study. We see these skills as underpinning the use of any of the type of skills covered in the next part.

Part B: Specific skills (Units 4–11)
Units 4–11 develop specific study skills needed for different kinds of study – following lectures, taking part in discussions, using the library, writing notes, and so on. These skills are introduced in such a way as to draw on and further develop skills of the type focused on in Part A.

Part C: Study practice (Units 12–15)
These units consist of four major study simulations, each of which is designed to consolidate and give further practice in applying the skills introduced in Units 1–11.

Part D: Study information
This part consists of:
1 a *Study Skills Profile* for the student to assess her/his improvement in study skills attainment as s/he proceeds through the book;
2 a *Glossary of Study Terms*, i.e., a list of expressions commonly used in study;
3 *Appendices* of task-related material, abbreviations and editing symbols;
4 a *Bibliography* of common reference books for study;
5 an *Index* of skills.

We regard Part A as essential for the kind of audience for which *Study Tasks in English* has been written. However, in our experience, students' needs with regard to the topics covered in the rest of the book are a good deal less predictable.

We have therefore tried to err on the side of comprehensiveness rather than narrowness, in terms of the range of topics covered. While we hope that the majority of users are likely to find the whole of the book of value, we have purposely designed it so that students only needing to improve specific skills can dip into it accordingly.

To this end, one of the aims of Unit 1 is to help students to evaluate their present knowledge of study skills in order to know how to make best use of the rest of the book. We also recommend that, throughout the use of the book, the teacher should provide for and encourage negotiation with the students about the choice, sequence and treatment (including adaptation) of the materials. It should also be noted that work involving Part C can be undertaken at any point when it is thought appropriate. There is no need to have gone all the way through Parts A and B first.

C: UNIT STRUCTURE

Parts A and B
Each unit in Parts A and B covers a set of skills related to a main topic (e.g., 'Asking critical questions').

Each of these units is divided into five main sections.

In each of the first four sections, a series of linked tasks is used to build up an understanding of a set of related skills.

In turn, where possible, these sections build progressively one on the other throughout the unit. (It should be noted that this is not always the case, since a skills-based syllabus does not always allow a neat and orderly progression. However, the skills within each of the sections of a unit are all always closely related to those in the other sections.)

Section 5 always takes the form of a *Unit assessment and application*, in which, through a further series of tasks, the students are helped to draw together and review the threads of the unit as a whole.

Part C
Each of the four units in this part involves extensive practice in applying the study skills focused on in the earlier parts, through a series of listening, speaking, reading and writing activities linked by a common academic topic.

Each of these units is divided into five main sections. In each of the first four sections, an aspect of the overall topic is focused on. The tasks in these sections simulate typical academic activities involving the subject matter, such as listening to a lecture, doing follow-up reading and then taking part in a seminar discussion.

Section 5 takes the form of a *Unit assessment*, in which students are encouraged to reflect on their performance in the work of the unit.

D: GETTING THE BEST OUT OF *STUDY TASKS IN ENGLISH*

i) Students' and teachers' roles

Study Tasks in English is intended for classroom use (rather than self-study). The tasks involve the learners in working on their own or in small groups. The role of the teacher is primarily that of a facilitator – managing time, helping students form groups, monitoring group work, helping the learners to assess their progress and needs, setting tasks, and so on. At all times students are required to play an active role in arriving at an understanding of what successful study in English involves.

We recognise that there will sometimes be pressures in the average teaching situation which will make it tempting for the teacher to adopt a more direct, 'telling' approach. However, while this may save time in the short term, the quality of long-term learning is likely to be lower, since the students will not have had an opportunity to think for themselves, to get accustomed to learning independently, and so on. Students need to understand this and other aspects of the rationale behind the approach adopted in *Study Tasks in English*. We therefore recommend that the teacher discusses this point with the students, in order to increase their understanding and, we hope, sympathy with the approach used.

ii) Guidance

A number of basic task types are used throughout *Study Tasks in English*. For example, students are frequently asked to reflect on what they already know about a given study topic, or what they feel they have learned about it after having done a series of tasks. On other occasions, the activities call for discussion with fellow students as part of the process of arriving at a clearer understanding of a study concept or technique. Other tasks involve analysis, decision making, problem solving and creativity of various kinds.

For students to carry out these tasks as effectively as possible, we recommend that appropriate guidance is provided. Thus, for example, the teacher should show the students how to do an unfamiliar activity by working through the first item with them, or by getting a group to model the process for the rest of the class, and so on. This is especially necessary for tasks which involve a way of working or mode of thinking which students may have had little or no exposure to in their previous education (such as co-operative small-group work or self-evaluation, for example). In such cases, try to anticipate potential problems and trouble-shoot them before, during and after the activity, as appropriate. This principle applies equally to subsequent encounters with similar activities, until students clearly show mastery of the processes involved, since it will rarely be the case that these are learned thoroughly enough after only one exposure.

iii) Academic subject matter

Many of the activities in *Study Tasks in English* involve making use of academic information as a vehicle for mastering the aspects of study in question. It is important to take into account student attitudes to and knowledge of academic content of this kind. Although the role of academic subject matter in *Study Tasks in English* is secondary, it is nevertheless essential that students understand and identify with it to the extent needed for carrying out the task in hand. To this end, it is important before introducing a task involving such information (e.g., in the form of a reading or listening passage) to check for any major factual, conceptual or linguistic gaps in the students' knowledge, and to remedy these appropriately. (It may also be the case that with certain groups of students it makes sense to substitute academic subject matter which is more appropriate in terms of interest, background knowledge and so on, and we recommend that this is done whenever necessary.)

It is also important to take into account the possibility that some students will not be motivated initially by some of the academic subject matter because they feel it is not related to their area of study. In such cases, it is worth pointing out that none of the subject matter in *Study Tasks in English* is highly specialised: it is intended to appeal to and be within the grasp of any student about to enter or already in higher education, regardless of their specialism. It is also usually the case that the work the topics relate to can be approached from a variety of perspectives (e.g., scientific, technological, humanities-oriented, etc.), thus providing scope for students from a wide cross-section of disciplines to contribute their knowledge and ideas. It might also be worth pointing out that, in any case, a wide-ranging interest in information of all kinds is a vital study skill in itself!

iv) Time

Many of the activities in *Study Tasks in English* involve discussion, reflection, preparation and so on, and all this takes time. We have already pointed out that we feel that this is time well spent – learning how to study effectively is a time-consuming process, and therefore there needs to be an adequate minimum amount of time set aside for this purpose. However, steps can be taken to use what time there is as efficiently as possible, as follows:

- assign as much work as possible to be done outside class (e.g., as homework): this encourages independence, as well as saving time;
- be selective in what you cover in *Study Tasks in English*: it is unlikely that every student will need to study all of the book;
- set time limits for small-group work, discussions and so on.

v) Knowledge

It is very important for the study skills teacher to be adequately prepared in terms of his/her own knowledge of what studying in English involves. Having had experience of English-medium higher education oneself is an important source of background information. However, this needs to be complemented by an understanding of the nature of the study process and how it can be learned. We therefore recommend that teachers who feel the need to expand their knowledge in this respect should consult the Bibliography of study skills books in the Students' Book (Part D).

Of equal importance is a knowledge of one's students – their study situations, their specialisms, and their perceptions about their study needs, both initially and as they progress. Study skills students are usually adults and will probably have clear views of their own about their priorities, and these obviously need to be taken into account. *Study Tasks in English* tries to create a context for finding out this kind of information and building on it. Thus the greater the interest the teacher has in his/her students' knowledge of and attitudes to study, the more he/she and they will get out of many of the activities in *Study Tasks in English*.

vi) Supplementation

No single book can of itself provide the student with all the knowledge and practice needed in order to prepare adequately for English-medium higher education. There is therefore every likelihood that the teacher will need to supplement some parts of *Study Tasks in English* with additional information and activities. Also, we strongly recommend that students undertake a programme of additional work involving application of the skills learned in *Study Tasks in English*. Only in this way are they likely to give themselves the degree of practice needed. Finally, it should once again be stressed that *Study Tasks in English* is not intended to cater to any significant extent for the language development needs of the learners. Additional material will therefore need to be provided for this purpose, as required.

UNIT **1** **How do I learn?**

The main aim of this unit is to begin to build up the students' awareness of what learning involves, particularly their knowledge of themselves as learners. The unit therefore introduces the learners to some of the basic resources needed for study, the factors that tend to affect success or failure in learning, some basic study management techniques, and an understanding of what they already know about studying and what they still need to learn. In addition, at the end of the unit, the students are encouraged to form a set of personal interim 'study targets'.

1.1　The aim of this task is to familiarise the students with *Study Tasks in English* while introducing skills such as skimming, scanning, and discussion techniques.

1.2　It is helpful for students to keep a record of their assignments and new words in addition to organising their class work and notes for future reference. Exactly how these are organised is up to the teacher and student. What is important is that the records and papers are kept in such a way that they are easily accessible to the student.

2.1–2.5　These tasks are intended to encourage students to consider how they learn best and then how they can use this knowledge in order to develop independent learning strategies.

2.2　It is important to probe and question the students as necessary in order to establish major points about the factors affecting effective learning, e.g., it is not simply a matter of having a good teacher or possessing the necessary capabilities. Students should also be encouraged to discuss and question what is meant by words such as *motivation*, *cleverness* and *success*, or what makes a topic 'interesting', in order to get a deeper and more detailed picture of the factors involved.

2.3   This activity will be more effective if the students are given paper and coloured markers to make interesting, expressive posters for their 'recipes'. Please note that making posters may well not be a requirement for the study situation the students are preparing for. However, that is not the intention. Rather, it is to provide the students with an activity that will help them to build up a 'rich picture' (i.e., a concrete and memorable image) of their ideas. We recommend that, if possible, the students' posters are put on display in the classroom until they have sunk in.

2.4   Some possible sample answers:
– Know as much as possible about what helps – and what hinders – your learning.
– Know your own strengths and weaknesses as a learner.
– Take positive, concrete action to improve your weaknesses.
– Be aware of all the resources available to you for learning, and use them as effectively as possible.
– Be clear about what you already know and can do.

2.5   Students unfortunately often do not reflect about why they have enrolled in a particular course or what they hope to gain from it beyond 'the government sent me' or 'I need a qualification'. However, it is obviously important that students learn to think about what they will be learning and doing on a course, and how it will meet their own needs, if they are to take responsibility for their learning. This fore-knowledge can prevent a lot of heartache at a later time, and help students come equipped with the right prior knowledge and skills. It also means they arrive confident in knowing what to expect and what they intend to learn – and this knowledge gives them some control over their own learning. It may be worth developing some of these points with your students beyond the actual task. Please also note that before they begin to answer the questions in this task, the students may need to investigate their course in order to find out who it is intended for, what previous knowledge and experience is required, what the course aims and syllabus are, and so on, and time will need to be allowed for this (preferably as homework).

3.1–3.5   Rather than telling students that they should study in a quiet place, get enough sleep and so on (which is not true for all students in any case), the aim of these tasks is to encourage students to look critically at their own study habits in order to see where and how they could be improved if necessary. Discussion is a critical element in this process and should be encouraged with leading questions from the teacher if necessary.

3.3   The introduction to this activity is not intended to imply that time problems are always the student's fault. For example, it may be that the student is taking too many classes and needs to drop some. Or pressing personal problems beyond the student's control may be a factor. However, research shows that poor time management by students is probably the single biggest cause of difficulty in higher education (see Student's Book page 189). This is not really surprising when you consider that it is probably this element of study – the independent management of one's time – which is more difficult than any other for the student to have experience of beforehand.

3.6

Note If students are currently involved in non-study activities (e.g., work) during most of the week, it will not be possible to do this task in detail. However, it may still be fruitful to have a general discussion of the issues involved.

The type of study plan focused on is only a suggestion, and students may choose to use one they feel suits their needs better. Some students may argue that they cannot keep to a study plan. We sympathise with this position, as neither author writes or follows such a plan, though both do work to some sort of routine. However, we would argue that the process of thinking the week through should be part of the critical examination of study practices which the students undergo. Whether or not students continue to make up and keep to a study plan is essentially a personal matter. However, those students who have difficulty managing time and continually have difficulty completing their work on time might be well advised to establish a study routine and attempt to keep to it.

4.1–5.3   The aim of these tasks is to introduce some of the skills involved in successful study in order to help students assess where they need to focus their study in this course. For students who are not working straight through *Study Tasks in English*, this should help guide them to those parts of the book that are most relevant to their own needs.

4.3   It is important that the students do not feel demoralised by this activity. They should be reminded that they have probably discovered that they already know a lot more than they realised they did. In any case, the main point is *not* that one needs to learn a very large number of techniques, but rather that one should develop the habit of critically assessing what one does and does not know in relation to the task in hand, with a view to taking into account any *major* shortcomings.

Note This activity also provides a good opportunity to introduce the students to the *Study Tasks in English* Study Skills Profile (page 194). This is a list of all the skills covered in *Study Tasks in English*, grouped into general categories (such as 'information-processing skills'), and referenced by Task. The Profile also includes a self-evaluation grid which students can use to assess the relevance of each of the skills to their study situation, their current knowledge of each of the skills and their progress in mastering them as they proceed through the course. The Profile can be photocopied for normal classroom use. We recommend that the students are introduced to the Profile by having their attention drawn to each of its main features, and discussing their value. They should be urged to use it regularly on an independent basis (this will need to be checked on from time to time), and we also suggest that you use it with the class at the beginning and end of each unit as a way of introducing and reviewing the work.

5.3   It may be that students are initially reluctant to do this activity, or do not do it very well. This is to be expected, however, as it may be the first major independent task of this kind that many of the students have been involved in. The point is that it involves not just the drawing up of the targets but, more fundamentally, a re-orientation of responsibility for determining learning away from the teacher and towards the learner him/herself. This needs patience, perseverance, support and encouragement, and is an attitude shift that cannot be expected to occur overnight. Thus, it may not matter too much if results are not initially impressive on the surface. The really important point is to make a beginning which goes in the right direction. It may help to discuss this point with the students. In any case, as indicated in the Student's Book, the targets should be regularly reviewed, in order to develop and refine them further.

UNIT **2** **Thinking it through**

The aim of this unit is to foster critical thinking skills involving asking
questions, considering alternatives and recognising different perspectives.

Section 1

The aim of this part of the unit is to give the students direct experience of
their existing ability to ask critical questions about study data and to identify
areas in which they need to improve this skill. The aim is *not* that of language
development often associated with the use of a table of this kind (*not* e.g.,
Japan is cooler than Kenya).

The procedure is deliberately inductive in order to provide the necessary
depth of learning. It is therefore vital for the teacher to play as indirect a role
as possible.

Encourage your students to involve themselves in processing the data as
realistically as possible. They should play the role of geography students
regardless of their specialism, as no specialist knowledge is needed. It also
needs to be emphasised that students should look for conclusions from the
table as a whole and not from just parts of it, as far as possible.

It should be noted that the table has been artificially constructed from
random data. All the information is authentic, but it did not appear together
in the way it is presented here, nor, as a consequence, was it originally
intended to yield any particular conclusion. In fact, the data has been
deliberately selected in order to make it impossible to draw any single,
unqualified conclusion from the table. This encourages depth of processing
and puts all the students in the same position, i.e., none is unfairly
advantaged due to specialist knowledge. However, please note that this
background information is provided for the teacher's benefit only. It is
crucial for the students to be given the opportunity to approach the table as
they would in real life.

1.1   The teacher should not tell the students what questions they should
ask, nor should s/he help the students arrive at a conclusion. It is important
that they be allowed to attempt to think it through for themselves, and if they
do make mistakes, they will be able to learn from these in Task 1.2. When
they have finished, elicit the groups' conclusions and note them down for
later reference.

1.2   In this activity, first find out what questions the students asked, and
then what further questions they felt they should have asked. If it turns out to
be the case that questions such as those which follow have not been thought
of by the students, then the teacher should present them and get the students

to say whether or not they are also important to take into account, and why:
- *What does temperate mean?*
- *How are nationality and population determined?*
- *When were these statistics taken?*
- *How was the information gathered?*
- *Who collected the information?*
- *Where was the information printed?*
- *Why were these countries selected?*
- *How are average earnings determined?*
- *What are we expected to find or do?*

If the students feel that any or all of these questions are not important, get them to explain the reasons for their views – do not simply tell them that you think they should have taken them into account. Try to steer them towards understanding why such questions are vital to critical thinking. Often students feel such questions should not be asked if the material has been given to them by a lecturer or is presented by a reputable authority. However, it is also important for the students not to feel overly discouraged or defensive because they did not consider these questions initially. You could point out to them that most people don't!

1.3a   In this activity, first find out what questions the students say they asked at this stage. If the following ones were not included, the teacher should present them, and then follow the same procedure as recommended for Task 1.2:
- *Where does the United Arab Emirates receive its wealth from?*
- *Why might Guinea's life expectancy be low?*
- *What do Kenya and Guinea have in common that could account for the similarities?*
- *How are climate and health related?*
- *What do I already know about these countries?*
- *Do these statistics support or refute what I already know about the distribution of wealth? How? Why?*
- *What is meant by rich? Poor? Dense? Sparse?*

1.3b   For the reasons given in the note about Section 1, it is not possible to draw a single, unqualified conclusion from the data. You may wish to begin this stage by going back to the record of the students' initial conclusions (see notes for 1.1) and asking them whether they would now like to modify them in any way.

1.4   This discussion is needed to encourage independent learning, and hopefully awareness of the importance of the need to ask critical questions in other areas of study. Critical questioning of this sort involves the self-confidence to question accepted facts and conclusions. Part of the teacher's role is to foster this self-confidence, as it is easy for this set of tasks to lead students to the conclusion 'I can't question' simply because they have not done so in the past, and this would be counter-productive. It may help to point out that asking critical questions does not involve specialised knowledge, and the questions are all in a form the students are already accustomed to. What is needed, therefore, is 'simply' a realisation of the need to ask the questions. The students should not blame themselves for any previous lack of awareness of this need: this is likely to be due to differing socio-educational traditions.

2.1   There is no single set of right or wrong answers here. Rather, the students should evaluate each other's questions in terms of factors such as relevance, breadth, depth and so on.

2.3a   Introduce the students to the plan of the school and to any key vocabulary and concepts in the dialogue which may be unfamiliar. To help them identify the factors, you may wish to have them first of all answer factual questions such as the following:
– *How are the areas around the school used at the moment?*
– *What are their main features?*
– *How easy is it to get to and from the building to the areas?*
– *How many children are there in the school? What problem does this cause?*
– *What are the two main problems the teachers are concerned with?*
– *What is the head teacher's main concern?*
– *What state is the pavement in?*
– *What problem is there in the area where the school is located?*
– *What kinds of children are there in the school?*
– *How many teachers are on duty at playtime?*
– *How much money is available?*
The students should then be able to use their answers to identify the main factors, namely, present use and condition of areas, access, children, noise, mud, supervision (during and after school), local conditions, finance.

2.3   Sample solution

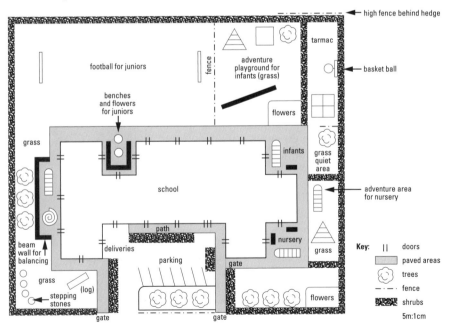

2.4 This task is designed to reinforce further the concept that questioning is an on-going process and not one that is just done at the beginning of an assignment.

3.1 There is no one set of answers for these terms. Students should write the definitions and word associations on their own before they compare answers (in order to avoid any tendency for ideas to agree too closely). If a group does not appear to have divergent meanings, the teacher should ask the group to imagine other meanings and associations that could reflect a different point of view. It may also be helpful for the teacher to ask them to discuss how different people or groups they have heard of or read about use these words, and why.

Note It is difficult to provide a set of words which will suit all situations in terms of culture, time available and so on. You should therefore feel free to select from and/or add to the list provided as appropriate.

3.2 It is important that this task is done in discussion form, not just written. As can be seen from the possible answers that follow, the answers are not straightforward and involve defining and questioning skills. We recommend that you work through the first one with the class, in order to provide a clear example of the reasoning processes involved.

1 'Support' can take many forms, and does not necessarily mean money. If the 'measures' are seen to relate to financial needs, support would mean money. However, if the 'measures' relate to organisation, re-allocation of resources, and so on, support could mean time, e.g., the speed at which the measures are carried out.

2 The problems here surround first what is meant by 'animal', and if 'animal' includes 'humans', and second, what is meant by 'language'. Some people see humans as unique or separate from the animal world. Others see humans as an extension of the animal world, and believe the things humans can do differ from other animals in quality, not in basic functions. Hence, human sounds and animal sounds are simply a matter of quality, not basic function. This quality might be defined as grammar, vocabulary, and so on, e.g., language. How is language to be defined?

3 Hans and Gloria may not agree on what is meant by the 'Third World', 'West', or 'better place'. More importantly, perhaps, they may be defining 'development' differently. If development means the West giving handouts to the Third World, they may in fact agree that development in this sense should stop without necessarily holding back 'progress', e.g., the advancement and fulfilment of the needs of most countries in the world.

4 'Thinking' is a complex word (and process), and one psychologists and philosophers have not agreed upon. Hiroko is perhaps thinking of computers programmed to perform or 'think' in the same way as the brains of animals do (or do animals think?). Hiroko seems to see thinking as putting two or more premises together to arrive at a conclusion (which may or may not be original). Mathematicians might feel that carrying out complex mathematical operations involves a kind of thinking, but computers carry out these operations faster and more accurately than the mathematician. Sorin, on the other hand, seems to define 'think' as something you cannot teach or tell someone or something how to do – a

kind of discovery process that cannot be replicated. In this sense, thinking is a unique, individual activity that cannot be dissected or analysed. Sorin may also be thinking of older computers that can only follow simple programmes involving basic, relatively linear instruction.

5 Noemi doesn't define 'think', and Ali assumes that she defines it as 'think logically'. This may or may not be the case. She may mean 'think about things, not people', 'think about parts, not the whole', or 'think about experiments'. She may, in fact, not know what she means, but until Ali knows, he is not really in a position to respond. His response is not logical in any case, as he may not be a representative sample of 'the rest of us'. He may be thinking 'as a scientist' about literature.

3.3   It is important to have the students first complete this exercise *individually*. Then, in groups, encourage the class to consider a wide range of possibilities, not pat answers. Here are a few possible answers or points for discussion.

1 *tall* – more than two storeys? More than ten storeys? Over 30 metres? Over 50 metres? Buildings tall enough to require steel structures? (Therefore all buildings with steel structures?)

2 *working-class* – people whose income is in the lower quarter of the population? Manual labourers? Unskilled labourers? Semi-skilled labourers? Unemployed? People whose parents called themselves 'working class'? Is it possible to be a working-class doctor or teacher (e.g., one whose parents were unskilled workers or someone who lives in poor housing)?

3 *large* – class with 100 members? 30 members? Ten members? Does the type of class affect the meaning of 'large' – e.g., pre-school children? Adults? Handicapped? Language classes?

4 *thin* – under 50 kg.? Under 70 kg.? How is height to be accounted for? How about bone structure? Under the recommended height/weight guidelines? 'In the eyes of the beholder' – (e.g., someone may consider themselves thin while a doctor may consider them overweight)?

5 *old* – more than 400 years old? More than 50 years old? Houses in poor repair? Houses without modern facilities?

4.1   Make sure the students understand the originals properly first of all.

1 By omitting that Wells states that Hitler was 'among the major reasons', the reference implies that Hitler was *the* chief cause of the war. Hence, it misrepresents Wells, who does not want to focus primarily on Hitler; the writer, in fact, wants to concentrate on Hitler. Possible summary: Hitler was only one of several major reasons for the Second World War.

2 The essay paraphrase omits examples and large or technical words. It is basically correct, however.

3 The original does not make a comparison between articulate and inarticulate individuals with regard to thinking ability. It is correcting/challenging the assumption that a correlation exists between articulation and thinking abilities. A better summary would state that de Bono indicates that the ability to verbalise ideas does not indicate the ability to think skilfully, nor is the reverse true either.

4.2   There are no single correct answers; students should be encouraged to consider the facts from as many perspectives as possible.

4.3   None is an absolute truth – even water boils at different temperatures depending on the pressure (or height above sea level). Some students, however, may hold them as absolutes, but as beliefs, not facts. In this case, they define 'truth' as an absolute belief divorced from 'facts', a point perhaps worth discussing.

4.4   This is a very important skill, as many students do not take enough time to consider the other side of the coin. It is important to stress that this does not mean that they have to change their minds – they may, or they may wish to modify their position. However, it could help strengthen their argument instead. The important thing is that the position is held for good reason, not simply impression or prejudice.

5.1   The analysis should include points such as the following:
- The purpose is clear, but inconsistent. The title gives the impression that the scope will be wider than it is, since, in fact, the context turns out to be only British.
- Key terms such as *health, not healthy, heart problems, British people* (which ones?) and *adults* (assumed to be equivalent to *12+?*) are not defined.
- One essential question which is not addressed is: 'What is the evidence linking heart disease and diet?'
- The table is not really relevant to the topic. The kind of table needed would be one which showed a correlation between diet and heart disease. On the other hand, the data from the UK DHSS is relevant to the topic.
- The author makes an unsubstantiated claim in the paragraph beginning 'British eating habits are changing . . . ' that the recent changes in the diet of British people are causing a reduction in heart disease.
- The author has failed to consider viewpoints which contradict his own, such as the findings of the DHSS survey.

UNIT **3** **Asking critical questions**

The aim of this unit is to develop further the critical thinking skills introduced in Unit 2 and to introduce cause–effect relationships, correlation, and causation.

Section 1

It may be necessary to begin by explaining that the setting of the introduction is the UK, where dogs typically live inside houses, and where letters are delivered to the house by a postman, who posts them through a letterbox in the outer door.

Deal with each of the main sections in the introduction in turn, ensuring the students have grasped each of the main points.

1.1 All the answers show faulty thinking.

a *If water is heated to 100°C, it boils.* – affected by pressure, altitude, purity of water.

b *If the fuel gauge points to empty, your motorbike will stop.* – unless the gauge is broken or you are going downhill.

   Note The bike will obviously stop for other reasons.

c *If you study hard, you will get a good result in your exams.* – affected by the quality of study, difficulty of exam, time given, etc.

   Note You may study hard and still not get good results and you may choose not to study and still get good marks.

d *If John is bitten by a malaria-carrying mosquito, he will have malaria.* – We know that if John has malaria, he must have been bitten by a mosquito.

   Note A qualification has been added to mosquito, as not all mosquitoes have this effect.

e *If a supermarket opens, the small shops will close.* – a tenuous argument that would need to be verified – the shops may have closed for other reasons.

f *If seat belts are worn, the number of deaths due to drunk driving will increase.* – obviously not a cause–effect relationship as the two events happen independently – simply a chance occurrence with no causal links beyond the statistical fact that both have occurred.

g *If inflation is high, wage demands will rise* or *If wage demands are high, inflation will be high.* – What is the cause and what the effect is debatable. There is no linear direction given between the two linked events; they may occur simultaneously without one directly causing the other, either by some third event causing both, by chance, or some cyclic causation in which both cause each other.

1.2   These are some of the possible answers:
1 blown light bulb; blown fuse; short in wire; a practical joker turning off the light switch; . . .
2 out of petrol; starter broken; you put the key in wrong; the engine is flooded; . . .
3 most role models are women; career prospects better for women; women more talented than men; most employers are men who like giving women orders; . . .
4 you did your sums wrong; you forgot to enter all your debits; the bank made an error; a friend borrowed your cheque card and withdrew money; . . .
5 too many students applied; your marks weren't high enough; you filled in the form wrongly; the secretary sent the letter to the wrong person; it wasn't your day; . . .
6 he/she got the wrong day; he/she doesn't like you; he/she lost your phone number; he/she is ill; . . .
7 you didn't study; the test was difficult; you are not good at maths; the exam was marked incorrectly; you broke a mirror before the exam; . . .
    Cultural note   In the UK, some people believe that breaking a mirror brings bad luck.
8 your friend is better in English than you; your friend studied more; your friend is lucky; your friend cheated; the teacher likes your friend more than you; . . .

1.3   1 shooting of Archduke Ferdinand by Gavrilo → 2 hatred between Serbians and Austrians → 3 Serbia colonised by Austria → 4 Serbia did not co-operate with Austria, so Austria declared war → 5 treaties between Russia, England, France, etc. → 6 justify/protect huge military investment → 7 capitalist greed

1.4   There is no correct answer, though the students should agree with the statement to some degree.

2.1b

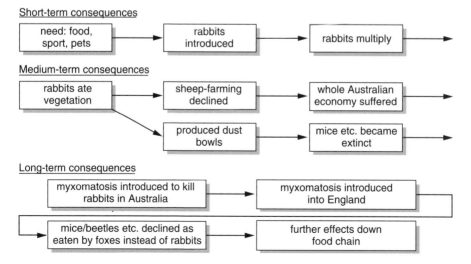

Short-term consequences

| need: food, sport, pets | → | rabbits introduced | → | rabbits multiply | → |

Medium-term consequences

| rabbits ate vegetation | → | sheep-farming declined | → | whole Australian economy suffered | → |
| | ↘ | produced dust bowls | → | mice etc. became extinct | → |

Long-term consequences

| myxomatosis introduced to kill rabbits in Australia | → | myxomatosis introduced into England |
| mice/beetles etc. declined as eaten by foxes instead of rabbits | → | further effects down food chain |

2.1c
1 for food, sport and as pets;
2 lack of experience, naiveté; short-sighted problem solving; ecology was not a science at that time; weak governmental controls; . . .
3 greed; indifference; ignorance; need for food; . . .

2.2 No set answers here – the aim is to encourage divergent thinking.

2.3 These exercises are not based on any experiments – the *r* values have been invented; in some instances, students are asked to invent probable *r* values.
1 The correlation indicates that smoking and lung cancer are linked, though this does not mean that an individual who smokes for twenty years will get lung cancer. However, statistically, he or she has a relatively high chance of getting lung cancer.
2 This is a weak correlation, just slightly better than chance. It is too weak to make any useful predictions.
3 Again, this is a weak correlation, even though it is negative. It indicates that people with a low IQ may have slightly less chance of earning a good income. (IQ and income are positively correlated.)
4 Between $r = 0.35$ and 0.65; income and family size have a relatively strong positive correlation.
5 Between $r = 0.65$ and 0.85; there is a high correlation between being apprehended for theft and going to prison.
6 Between $r = -0.65$ and -0.85; there is a high negative correlation between height and shade (sunflowers need sunlight to grow tall).
7 Depends on your point of view – if very weak (almost chance) then *r* will be between 0.00 and 0.20; if linked but not strongly, then *r* is between 0.20 and 0.35; if there is a strong link, then *r* is between 0.35 and 0.65.
Note Coefficients above $r = 0.85$ indicate a very strong relationship on which valid predictions can be based. However, only $r = 1.00$ correlations are certainties.

3.1 No set solutions – students should consider the probabilities of different outcomes occurring as well as what the alternative consequences of different courses of action may be.

3.2 No set solution – some students may wish to reject both plans, in which case they should try to develop a plan all three councillors (or at least two) can agree on.

3.3 There are no set answers. There follow some suggestions.
1 – If guns are possessed, they are more likely to be used.
  – People cannot be expected to act responsibly.
  – The good of the state should override the freedom of the individual.
2 – Women should be responsible for what happens to them.
  – Abortions promote the good health of the nation.
  – The foetus is not yet a living human being.
3 – Preventing death is more important than promoting individual freedom.
  – People will not act safely unless made to do so.

– It is the government's job to protect people from themselves.
4 – Students will not attend unless they are made to do so.
  – What is said in class is more valuable than what can be learnt independently in the library or elsewhere.
  – It is the institution's job to make people learn whether they want to or not.
5 – Public transport is essential for the improvement of the economy.
  – Transport is a public service, and a right, not a privilege.
  – Public funding will increase demand and services, leading to better efficiency.
6 – Health is an individual freedom, not a right of all citizens.
  – Competition will lead to a better service.
  – The public purse is not limitless, and should be reserved for those with the greatest need.

3.4

1 Joan.   2 James.   3 Joan.   4 James.   5 Joan.   6 Depends on how the terms are defined – animal life or human life?   7 Both.

4.1

1 No – opinion; it may be true but the only supported statement is that working women continue to fulfil their domestic duties whereas men do not.
2 Yes – it may not be better legislation that is needed but other kinds of support and education. However, if women receive lower wages for the same work, then there is a definite argument for better legislation, regardless of whether women feel discriminated against or not.
3 No – men and women tend to agree about this, but that may be because they accept the same values and have not tried reversing roles, for example.
4 Yes – the attitudes expressed by women which perceive men as better in science and humanities combined with women's perception that they haven't fulfilled their life's ambitions combine to support this conclusion.
5 Yes – if only 19% of the women feel they have fulfilled their ambitions, it could be argued this is because the opportunities aren't there – career opportunities require training, education, previous experience, etc.
6 No – perhaps men should be paid less – it is an opinion based on an assumption that wages should be equal for equal work, and that wages should always go up, assumptions we may agree with, but none the less, assumptions.

4.2   There are lots of examples of faulty logic and jumping to conclusions in this letter – weather, food, all British universities the same, no exams, etc.

4.3

1 English will definitely be studied in any type of higher education. John is going to be doing higher education. It therefore follows logically that John will have to study English.
2 The apple in question may or may not be green, since worms are attracted to sweet apples, but sweet apples may be red or yellow in colour, not just green. The conclusion is therefore illogical.

3 The conclusion is illogical, since it assumes that tall teachers are automatically good teachers, which is obviously false.
4 The conclusion is logical.
   Note One may not agree with hanging convicted murderers, but that is not the issue here, which is only to do with the correctness of the logic, not the ethics or morality of the matter.
5 This argument is faulty because it a) ignores the *most* b) reverses the original argument to become *people who write books are clever*.
6 Illogical, since if it is only some lessons in which the scarves are dangerous, it is illogical to ban them from being worn in all lessons, which is what forbidding them to be worn in school amounts to.

4.4   In the answers that follow, *Pa* and *Pb* are the premises and *Con* is the conclusion.
2 *Pa:*   All pilots have fast reflexes.
  Pb: Jack has fast reflexes.
  Con: Jack will be a good pilot.
     *illogical – to be logical, *Pa* should read:
     All people with fast reflexes make good pilots.
3 *Pa:*   People who study hard are good students.
  Pb: Maria is a good student.
  Con: Maria studies hard.
     *illogical – it is only logical if *Pb* and *Con* are reversed:
     Maria studies hard, therefore she is a good student.
4 *Pa:*   Children who have never been hit are naughty.
  Pb: James is naughty.
  Con: James has never been hit.
     *illogical – *Pa* makes no mention of children who have been hit; perhaps they are naughty as well.
5 *Pa:*   Some chemically grown vegetables are dangerous.
  Pb: Organically-grown vegetables do not use chemicals.
  Con: Organically-grown vegetables are not dangerous.
     *illogical – *Pa* makes no mention of vegetables grown without chemicals. They may be even more dangerous for all that is stated here.
6 *Pa:*   More channels will offer more choice.
  (*Pb* is assumed: each channel will be different.)
  Con: There will be more choice.
     *illogical – this is only logical, and true, if *Pb* is substantiated. However, it is not stated in the problem, so as it stands, it is not logical.
7 *Pa:*   Good students go to bed early.
  Pb: Leela will go to bed early.
  Con: Leela will be a good student.
     *illogical – other people besides good students may go to bed early. To be logical, *Pa* would have to read:
     People who go to bed early are good students.
8 *Pa:*   Anything well-known experts say is always true.
  Pb: A well-known expert said this.
  Con: It is true.
     *logical – though *Pa* is not true.

UNIT **4** **Finding information**

The aim of this unit is to encourage students to find the information they require independently by exploring different sources of information available in most libraries and by using catalogues and bibliographies to locate the sources relevant to their needs.

1.1   Many people associate books with libraries. This task looks at the different kinds of printed material available that students may need to use as references. Students need to explore and share the information they already know about books in libraries. Some vocabulary such as *abstracts* and *journals* may be unfamiliar to all the class members. If this is the case, the teacher may need to supply examples or definitions.

1.2   This task looks at services offered in libraries in addition to the references mentioned above. Mano mentions the following services: 1, 4, 5, 7, 8, 9, 10, 15, 16 and 17. Students should be aware of what services might be available in order to know what kinds to look for in the different libraries they may use in the future.

1.3   If there is no library available, you may have to omit this exercise. It is helpful, however, to explore a library, even if it isn't in English, to find out what the different references and sources look like and how they can be used effectively.

1.4   It is unlikely that the libraries you are using will have either of the two systems mentioned here, though they will probably use something similar to one of them. It is important students are aware of the differences and how the books are located in each. Students who have difficulties using the system in a library should feel confident about asking the librarian for help. Many universities and other higher education institutions offer guided tours to new students.

1.5
1 *Freedom to Study* has two authors: Jean Hutton and Bruce Reed. It is located at JSea.MN in the library. This is found by first finding where J is located, then JS and then finding the remaining letters alphabetically on the shelves. Line 6 of Card 1 mentions a third author, although only the first two are cited in the first part of the card. However, the card is authentic: this is exactly the way the original was. You may wish to draw the students' attention to this, and point out that this example illustrates that the world of real-life study may sometimes contain puzzles of this kind. Students should therefore 'expect the unexpected'.

2 The subject is History of Accounting. The title of the book is *Interest as a Cost*, by Clinton H. Scovell. It is located at TQH.

3 The title is *Female soldiers: combatants or non-combatants?* This is a collection of articles edited by Nancy L. Goldmen. It was published by Greenwood Press in 1982. It is located at RMOW.

4 *From Dickens to Hardy* was edited by Boris Ford. Its ISBN is 0 14 020413 X. It is the sixth book in the Pelican Guide to English Literature series published by Penguin.

1.6a   One of the main difficulties in using a card or computer catalogue is deciding what to look up – especially if you are looking for information on a specific topic. This is the problem John and Mary discuss.

1.6b

1 advertising, charities, fund-raising activities, . . .
2 world leaders, 20th century politics, under the names of some world leaders, . . .
3 ecological disasters, rabbit, Australian animals, . . .
4 investments, auctions, names of some art treasures, . . .
5 children's reading, learning psychology, . . .
6 World Bank, International Monetary Fund (IMF), Third World Development, . . .

2.1   This task is intended as an introduction to the parts of a book (and essay or dissertation). Students should discuss the function and layout of each section.

2.2

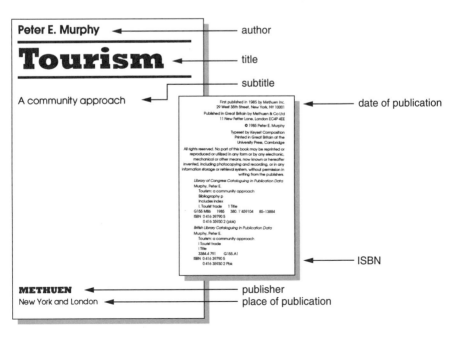

2.3   These are possible answers; the justification for the answer is more important than the actual answer.
1 Chapter 10.
2 No, though issues may be found in Chapter 11.
3 Chapters 6 and 7.
4 Possibly Chapter 2.
5 Possibly Chapter 3; Chapters 8 and 9.
6 Possibly Chapter 3; Chapter 11.
7 Possibly Chapters 6 and 7.
8 Possibly Chapters 1 and 3.
9 Possibly Chapter 1.
10 Possibly Chapters 4 and 5.

2.4   We have listed a variety of possible words for where the information could possibly be found, and have **highlighted** the word(s) to look up in the index provided (i.e., for the words needed for Task c). The page numbers are in brackets.
1 **population growth**, birth rate (Murphy: 27; 81)
2 parks, land use, cost effectiveness, **safari parks**, wildlife parks, zoos (Murphy: 148)
3 **REKA** (Murphy: 23)
4 parks, earnings, **recreation, as industry**, tourist industry, improvement, revenue, **recreation areas, class of visitors** (Cheek and Burch: 232–235, 50–51)
5 train travel, transport, infrastructure, railways, stations, **railway travel** (Murphy: 18)
6 recreation and play distinguished, play vs. recreation, play, recreation, recreation as play, play as recreation, **recreation, defined, play, defined** (Cheek and Burch: 7–8)
7 occupations, jobs, activities, socio-economic groups, **occupations, and life-style, and outdoor activities** (Cheek and Burch: 54–71, 58–59)
8 outdoor recreation, **outdoor activities, and education**, tourism and education (Cheek and Burch: 51–53)
9 elderly, **package tours**, over 60s, senior citizens, old age pensioners (OAPs), retirement, **retirement market** (Murphy: 24; 156)
10 **Olympic games**, international games, sports, athletics (Cheek and Burch: 212)

2.5   This task is intended as a summary of this section, with the aim of cementing the information in Task 2.1.

1 c, f; 2 b, h, i; 3 a, b, i; 4 g; 5 e; 6 d; 7 c, f, g; 8 c.

3.1

1 journals; 2 both; 3 journals; 4 journals; 5 textbooks, sometimes journals also; 6 both; 7 textbooks; 8 both; 9 both; 10 textbooks.

3.2   These are possible answers; students may be able to justify a different order, or suggest an alternative method of obtaining the information.

1 e; 2 a; 3 f; 4 d; 5 c; 6 b.

3.3
1 maps of countries, currents, ocean depths, contour maps; population data; weather data, etc.
2 definitions of words, information about how words are used; abbreviations; synonyms; antonyms, etc.
3 details about places; how things work; what famous people achieved, etc.
4 list of books printed in any year; where printed; by whom, etc.
5 synonyms and antonyms, word families, words with related meanings, etc.

3.4   Each card gives the author, title, publisher, date of publication, index number, and card code. Information about the book and details/notes have been omitted. The card codes are important as they save repeatedly writing out the information.

4.1a
1 *Much is Taken, Much Remains*
2 1973
3 Duxbury Press
4 North Scituate, Mass. (USA)
5 *Tourism and Development*
6 second edition
7 London
8 1977

4.1b   The information in this bibliography is indicated in the following ways. However, students should be encouraged to notice differences in ways of presenting this information in other bibliographies.
1 bold print; last names first, then initials; alphabetically by the last name
2 last entry in each reference, preceded by the place of publication
3 in brackets after the authors, in bold print
4 after the title, followed by a comma, and then the publisher
5 listed alphabetically (unless one author wrote the majority of the book), connected by **and**
6 (ed) or (eds) appears after the author(s) but before the date of publication; directly before the title where the reference is taken from another book.

4.2a
1 1980
2 46, pp. 145–53
3 'Too many Americans out in the wilderness'
4 *Geographical Magazine*, Volume 47, Issue 8
5 Volume 31, Issue 3

4.2b
1 in quotation marks after the date
2 in italics after the title of the article
3 in brackets after the author name(s)
4 after the name of the journal, followed by a comma and either the issue or page numbers
5 the last numbers in the reference

4.3
1 article in a book of collected works
2 book or pamphlet
3 article in a book of collected works
4 article written for a conference presentation (speech) – collection of papers
5 article in a newspaper
6 article in a book of collected works

4.4   There are many differences, especially in punctuation. These are some of the major similarities: alphabetised by author's surname; all contain the author, title of article or book, date of publication, and publisher or name of publication – i.e., enough information to relocate the source if necessary.
   Specific points:
1 Authors may be in bold, indented, or not indicated in any special way.
2 Date of publication may be after the authors or after the publisher.
3 The title may be underlined or in italics, or in quotation marks.
4 The publisher may be in parentheses.
5 The place of publication may be omitted.

4.5
1 author, date in brackets, title of book, place of publication, publisher, *or* title of chapter/article, title of book/journal, with place of publication, publisher for a book but not a journal, page numbers
2 e.g., (1977a) (1977b)
3 the one written earlier
4 the one whose surname comes earlier in the alphabet
5 alphabetically under the first word of the committee name (e.g., Countryside Commission)

4.6   Make sure that whatever format a student chooses, it is adhered to throughout the bibliography. The sources should be listed in alphabetical order, by author surname.

5.1a
1 Unit 5
2 multiple-choice, short answer, essay, and project work or extended research
3 Yes – writing good notes requires active thinking.
4 Unit 5.2.2
5 *r*
6 listen actively, prepare, take notes, ask questions, . . . (see Unit 6)
7 two or more circles linked together to show membership of groups (Unit 3.4.3)
8 ibid. means 'in the same place' (of a reference – in the work just mentioned)

UNIT **5** **Taking and making notes**

The overall aim of this unit is to expose students to a variety of techniques for note-taking, and to give them opportunities for putting the techniques into practice. Section 1 begins by examining what makes good notes, using a variety of layouts. The aim is to show the student that there is no one best way to take notes: the layout will vary with the student, the purpose and the content. The importance of adopting an active frame of mind when taking notes is also stressed. Some of the mechanics of note-taking (e.g., use of abbreviations) are touched on. Section 2 provides opportunities to practise these principles and techniques in the context of taking notes from written sources, while Section 3 covers the additional skills involved in taking notes while listening. Section 4 covers techniques for locating and combining notes from a variety of sources as part of preparing an academic assignment.

1.1   Note-taking can help you organise your thoughts, help you follow the argument of the speaker or writer, record details as well as the gist of a presentation, remember what was presented for a greater length of time, . . .

1.2b   You will need to provide students with the following list of characteristics of good notes. Students may wish to add or modify these in groups.
1 They are accurate.
2 They contain the essential information only: they are not too detailed, or too brief.
3 They show the overall organisation of ideas clearly.
4 They are concise, i.e., they use abbreviations and other techniques for shortening information whenever possible.
5 They help you listen or read more successfully.
6 You can use them effectively later on, e.g. for exam revision.
7 They include follow-up points, i.e. your own comments on or reactions to ideas.

1.3   The topic which each set of notes is concerned with should be briefly introduced first of all. It should be noted that there is no necessary one-to-one relationship between the organisation of the information in the texts and the type of note-taking layout used. Rather, the point is that the more students know about the range of possible layouts, the more flexible the choices at their disposal.

Example	Kind of note	Information being recorded	Main features
a)	linear and pattern	3 main ideas about how languages originated	• indentations • tree diagrams • symbols • abbreviations • headings
b)	pattern	main types of waves in the electromagnetic spectrum, and some of their features	• spider-web diagram
c)	pattern and linear	arguments for and against killing a certain kind of whale	• table/chart
d)	linear and pattern	Maslow's hierarchy of types of human need and examples of each	• flow chart (hierarchical table)
e)	linear	reasons for collapse of communism in E. Europe and the former Soviet Union	• numbering • indentation • headings • abbreviations

1.5   Writing personal comments in notes is often an aspect overlooked by students. However, it is important if active learning is to occur. If students have their own books, underlining and making personal notes in the margins is often a good way to simplify note-taking. Above all, students need to be encouraged to see note-taking as an active process, both in the sense of detecting and/or imposing a framework on information (the main concern of the earlier tasks in this section), and in the sense focused on here, i.e., striving to link the information in the book, etc. or lecture to the student's existing knowledge and views.

1.6b   Suggested abbreviations:

1 =; 2 approx. or c.; 3 ≠; 4 esp.; 5 e.g.; 6 cf.; 7 C; 8 ∴; 9 no. or # (US);
10 ≡; 11 ∴; 12 i.e.; 13 NB; 14 >; 15 °; 16 →; 17 <; 18 re.; 19 ≈; 20 + or &

1.7   Information missing:
1 author, page number(s)
2 author's initials, actual title of talk, date of lecture (and place if appropriate)
3 author's initials, title of article or book, publisher, page number(s)
4 author's initials, publisher, date of publication
   If students have difficulty with this exercise, they should be referred (again) to Unit 4, Task 3.4. Good reference notes have the source card information (or simply the source card reference) plus the page(s) from which the notes were taken.

2.1a   Possible points for improvement:
1 numbering inconsistent

2 omits details such as:
  a) gases (produced by burning trees, . . .) trap the heat which then creates
     the problems
  b) percentage of CO_2 is 56%, much greater than the CFCs which are noted
3 abbreviations hard to follow, inconsistent, and often incorrect
4 although he makes personal comments, these are infrequent and not clear
5 omits source/reference for information
(This list is not comprehensive.)

2.2–2.3   There is no one correct way to answer as the aim is to put all the
points for making good notes into practice. It is worth reminding students
that highlighting is a good practice after they have taken notes, simply as a
way to revise, evaluate and consolidate the information.

3.1a   Possible answers:
1 This may involve speeding up or slowing down. Speeding up typically
   occurs when recapping; when going over something less important; when
   running out of time! Slowing down may occur when introducing a new
   point, especially one which is important or complex. The main reason for
   varying speed is thus to say something about the status of the information
   being conveyed.
2 This typically occurs when introducing a new section or point, or ending
   one, or, if the section/point is lengthy, in the middle of it, in order to
   remind the listener of the drift. The main reason for doing so is to help the
   listener be clear about the overall structure of the talk, the connection
   between the main points, etc. Also, good speakers always build in plenty of
   redundancy, to allow for inattention, failure to grasp the point the first
   time round, etc.
3 Gestures, changes in position and so on are typically used to add emphasis,
   signal a new point/section, indicate the level of importance of the
   information, and so on. This enables the speaker to add meaning beyond
   the words themselves.
4 All sorts of visual aids may be used, from blackboard sketches to overhead
   projector transparencies to videos. It is important for students to realise
   that the diagram, etc. may be used by the lecturer to carry the majority of
   the meaning, and verbal language used on these occasions will not usually
   be self-sufficient – rather, it will be important to interpret it in close
   relation to the visual. Lecturers use visuals mainly in order to communicate
   relations between ideas, to express information which is not easily
   transmitted just by words, and so on.
5 By 'set expressions' is meant any of the myriad of words and phrases which
   speakers use to introduce and divide up their points, and draw points/
   sections to an end. These are used to make these transition points clear, so
   that the listener can better follow the overall connections between points.
6 Other possible non-verbal clues might include facial expressions,
   intonation, and bodily posture. Any cross-cultural differences in these
   should be clarified. They are used to add meaning: to emphasise, to
   indicate importance, to 'punctuate', and so on.

3.2   There is no one set answer here – students should make a case for the method of organisation of their choice. Some suggestions:
1 Types of motivation – linear
2 How a computer understands a program – flow chart
3 Theory X and Theory Y Managers – table
4 Population control – flow chart
5 World religions – spidergram

4.2–4.3   The intention of these activities is to give practice not just in making but also in *using* notes, by simulating the essentials of a typical academic task, i.e., synthesising a range of ideas on a topic, and then putting forward one's own viewpoint.

5.1   Students can be encouraged to contribute their own items to the list.

UNIT 6 Coping with extended English

The aim of this unit is to help students develop strategies and techniques for coping with the large amounts of spoken and written English they will need to be able to handle in their studies. The emphasis is on the need to adopt an active, questioning, thinking approach to this aspect of study, as practised in previous units, as well as to learn how to make efficient use of techniques such as skimming and scanning, using context clues, predicting, etc.

1.1a   Students may refer to their mother tongue reading habits if they lack experience of extensive reading in English.

1.1c   It is vital that students justify their views. It should emerge that effective reading for academic purposes requires an active, self-reliant, questioning approach on the part of the reader, which relates what is being read to what the reader already knows, the task in hand, etc. Students should therefore adopt strategies that help them to adopt such an approach, and try to avoid those which do not. Research shows that behaviours of the kind represented by the *odd-numbered* statements in 1.1a are generally those of successful students (in terms of overall grades), whereas those represented by the even-numbered statements are generally associated with less successful students.
Note It is vital, however, for the students to come to understand this for themselves as far as possible, not simply be told.

1.2
1 They can't keep up.
2 They can't listen, think and write at the same time.
3 They can't keep their minds on what he is saying.
4 They can't follow the train of thought or how the ideas are connected.
5 The main points of the lecture are frequently forgotten.

1.3   As with most tasks, it is important for students to analyse their own habits and needs, in order to assess how best these can be improved. Usually this is done best by working in small groups.

2.1   One of the main aims of this book is to encourage an active approach to learning study skills. We would like to suggest these additional questions need to be asked for active learning.
4 What do I not know?
5 What do I think about the ideas?
6 What information do I hope to obtain?
7 How will I use the information?

2.2   We hope students take an active approach to reading *Study Tasks in English*. They should be asking questions similar to those in 2.1 continuously; these are on-going (hence active) questions.

2.3a   No single correct answer is possible, as students are predicting and therefore there must be room for error. This is what follows generally:
1 Historical account of the development of the concept of 'War Crimes'.
2 Expansion on the main reasons and practical consequences of each of two main views, firstly regarding those in favour of censorship, then regarding those against; general conclusion trying to find a middle way.
3 The others attempt to clarify their points in response to Linda's questions.

2.3b
1 is from Task 6.4.3a; 2 is from 7.1.3a; 3 is from 7.3.4.

2.4a   Before doing this task, ensure the students understand what is meant by the various patterns of organisation (comparison/contrast, etc.). Students should briefly justify their answers, i.e., say what it is about the topic or its possible treatment that would involve the type of organisation in question.

1 d, i, j; 2 a, c, e, j; 3 b, h; 4 b, d, j; 5 c, g; 6 a, b, e; 7 g, j, k, l; 8 e, g; 9 a, e, j; 10 b, g, i; 11 b, d, g; 12 b, f, j; 13 f, g, i, j; 14 a, g, j, k, l; 15 j, k, l; 16 a, d, h, i, j.

2.4b   Page 61: b, c, f, j; pages 82–3: b, e. Let the students discuss their ideas.

2.5
1 poor machine design
2 design of workplace
3 unsafe systems of working
4 lack of training
5 inadequate supervision
6 environmental factors in the workplace
7 payment by results – pressure of increased productivity

3.1   Students may refer to any lecture or article written in English or their first language. The aim is self-analysis of efficient reading skills.

3.2
1 scanning 2 skimming 3 scanning 4 scanning 5 skimming 6 skimming
7 scanning 8 either – justify your choice

3.3
1 main ideas 2 main ideas 3 specific details 4 specific details 5 main ideas
6 specific details 7 specific details 8 main ideas 9 main ideas 10 specific details 11 either – depending on the question being asked 12 main ideas

3.4a

Note There can obviously be no one right answer here.
Para 1: Greenhouse effect is today's biggest problem. What are its causes?
Para 2: The main cause is over-production of gases which trap heat, thus raising atmospheric temperature.
Para 3: We are currently suffering from the effects of greenhouse gases released in the past. Greater future harm is likely to be caused by further releases.
Para 4: Rising global temperatures will mean extensive flooding.
Para 5: Another effect will be smaller harvests.
Para 6: Ocean currents may change course.
Para 7: Warmer temperatures release more CO_2, which in turn increases temperatures: will this 'chain reaction' become uncontrollable?

3.4b

– facts and figures: cost, compulsory schooling, no. of pupils, schools, etc.
– nos. of higher education institutions and students
– the National Curriculum and the examination system
– average primary/secondary class size
– rates of pay of primary/secondary teachers

3.5a

1 carbon dioxide and chlorofluorocarbons (CFCs) (key words: *two main gases*)
2 more than half a degree (key words: *world's temperature risen*)
3 3° C (key words: *temperatures rise to, 2070*)
4 20% (key words: *rainfall, in Sahara, fall*)
5 10° C to 12° C (key words: *temperature, rise, poles*)

3.5b

1 5 to 16 years (key words: *age, compulsory schooling*)
2 77 universities (key word: *universities*)
3 GCSE and A levels (key words: *secondary, examinations*)
4 1:22 (key words: *teacher:pupil ratio*)
5 about £18,000 (key words: *salary scale*)

3.5d   If the students still need further practice in this area, we would suggest getting them to do the following additional tasks:
1 In pairs, select two passages in textbooks for other classes. (If these are not available, use other passages in *Study Tasks in English*.) Write five questions for details in the passage for your partner to answer. Exchange questions and correct.
2 Were you able to answer your partner's questions? Were you able to look for key words and let your eye float along looking for these words? Were you able to complete the task quickly? Do you feel you have mastered this technique?

4.1   The list will vary between students; however, the list of words to look up in the dictionary should be relatively short.

4.2a

1 The job requires a higher level of competence than the employee has.
2 Because highly competent workers who are good at solving their job problems still suffer stress.
3 Because they show how people think about their work, and this influences their behaviour.
4 Because the way you see your job has a much deeper influence on your behaviour than mastering efficient job techniques.
5 Unsatisfactory conditions of service and excessively high self-expectations.
6 Institute regular mental health checks; use better job selection techniques; set more realistic goals.

4.3a

1 The main idea is the way in which the behaviour of soldiers in war has come to be controlled by the concept of 'war crimes', i.e., some types of behaviour have become illegal, even in war.
2 Since the reading has established some of the basic facts of the concept of war crimes, it would be reasonable to expect the lecture to move on to analysis, evaluation, etc., e.g., to be about the pros and cons of war crimes trials. Some further factual information might also be given, of course.
3 Possible questions:
   – What are war crimes?
   – What are the arguments in favour of the war crimes concept?
   – What are the arguments against the war crimes concept?
   – What are the practical procedures involving war crimes trials?
   – What are the problems of enforcing war crimes legislation?
   – What form might future war crimes legislation take?
   – What possible future improvements in procedures for enforcing war crimes legislation might there be?
   Students should give reasons for their predictions.
4 The point here is to identify the ones in the reading which are likely to come up in the lecture, and which would be crucial to understanding it. Some possible examples:

campaign	extermination
ill-treating	committed against
formal and comprehensive code	charges
discipline	lodged
responsible	genocide
commission	wanton destruction
outrages	hearings
categories of offence	acquitted
non-aggressive	sentenced
violations	convicted
hostages	tribunal

Note The actual words the students choose are less important than their reasons for doing so, i.e., why exactly it is that they think such-and-such a word is or is not likely to be crucial to understanding the lecture. It is also important to point out that the focus should be on words specific to this topic, rather than the myriad of more general words that could come up, regardless of topic!

4.4   Students should look at a variety of dictionaries and grammar books in order both to decide which they find most useful, and so as to know which best meets different purposes. It may be necessary to define symbols such as the parts of speech and phonetic symbols. Students may need additional exercises requiring the use of the dictionary. One way to do this is to repeat Task 4.1 using alternative texts, and then have students use their dictionaries or grammar books to look up the meaning and use of the essential words.

5.1   They share similar problems. These include:
– difficulty in coping with so much reading and extended listening;
– inappropriate reading strategies (therefore reading everything carefully and for details);
– taking very long, detailed notes (i.e., trying to write everything down);
– inability of the notes to convey the needed information when the students refer to them at a later time.

UNIT **7**   **Taking part in discussions**

The aim of this chapter is to help students to get the best out of academic discussions (seminars, etc.) by looking at a) how to prepare for discussions, b) how to present one's own point of view effectively, c) how to understand others' points of view in discussions, and d) how to contribute effectively to the management of the discussion.

1.1   Students may not have had much experience of discussion-based learning, so if this is the case it is worth beginning this section by first of all clarifying the nature of and role played by the typical seminar discussion in English-medium higher education.

Problems with discussions often stem from inadequate or ineffective preparation. Students often assume that because the work is oral, and in a group, they can't or needn't prepare in the same way that they would for written work, or for more individual oral work.

1.2   The strategy we recommend is that students should get into the habit not only of looking at their own point of view, but of trying to anticipate other viewpoints as well. This is an important part of the essence of most English-medium higher education, i.e., learning to think critically and independently. For students who come from socio-educational traditions where this is not the norm, we recommend taking the time to explain and discuss this point first of all.

1.3   Students also need to prepare for discussions by critically examining new ideas using the skills presented in Units 2 and 3. Readings should be actively read, and questioned before accepting, rejecting or qualifying the new ideas being presented. If necessary, refer back to these units.

1.4   The topic does not need to be related to their studies. It doesn't even need to be academic. If students have difficulty selecting a topic, you may wish to suggest several topics of local or national interest: should some change occur in the class or school, should local government take action about some immediate concern, etc.

2.1a–b   The skills involved here are far from just a matter of how good your English is. We feel that the argument against robots (i.e., Paul's one) is the weaker argument because:

1 The argument for robots clearly states its position and then gives the reasons that support this position. It takes into account arguments against robots, and it gives examples to support and clarify its position. It ends with a summary/paraphrase of the arguments that support the position.

2 The argument against robots is not clearly or logically organised. It does not directly address the question of employment but jumps between various emotive arguments concerned with the dehumanising effects of robots. It does not lead the listener through well thought-out, reasoned arguments. Instead, the listener only hears a jumble of generalisations and prejudices lacking support. The listener is left with no clear idea of what Paul's position is, or how it has been supported.

2.1c   Sample revised argument:
I believe that robots are likely to create fewer, not more jobs. My main reason for thinking this is that robots are so much more efficient at most jobs that employers will want to use them in ever-increasing numbers. Even if the use of robots leads to better, cheaper goods being produced, and this results in more jobs being created, these jobs will be taken over by robots as soon as possible, because they are able to do almost any job more efficiently. So the new jobs that robots may create will just provide employment for more robots, not humans, in the long run! Of course, some people argue that it is just certain kinds of jobs that robots will be used in more and more – the mechanical kinds of jobs, where not much thinking is involved, for example working on a factory assembly line, and so on. But this assumes that robots are only capable of jobs that don't require thinking. That might be true now, but in the future, as the computers that control robots become more and more complex, it is possible that robots will become much more intelligent, and become able to do jobs that involve thinking as well, such as teaching, flying aeroplanes, performing medical operations, and so on. And because they will be able to do those jobs more cheaply and reliably than humans, employers are certain to prefer them, so in this way as well robots will eventually lead to fewer and fewer jobs for people. So, to sum up, what I'm saying is that although robots may well produce more jobs, they won't necessarily be jobs for us – they're more likely to be for robots.

2.2   No set answer as the notes depend on the position the student takes. It is important that the students prepare the initial position before they hear the discussion so far. You may need to play the discussion more than twice if they are unable to record all the expressions.
Agreement:
– I'm all in favour of it.
Disagreement:
– I think both of you are looking at the matter much too narrowly.
– I think it's also vital to consider . . .
Both:
– I would agree with you up to a point, . . .
– but where I differ is about . . .
Other language worth noting if your students need the practice:
Paraphrasing:
– in other words, . . .
Example/Explanations:
– in fact, . . .
– after all, . . .
– so, . . .

3.1   Additional expressions are in brackets. If this exercise proves difficult, or if short of time, list the items on the blackboard beforehand (without the brackets), and have the students say which ones occur in the text.

Asking for clarification
- What exactly do you mean by . . .
- So you're saying that . . .
- So, just to make sure I've got this right . . .
- Can I just check a couple of things that still aren't clear to me . . .
- I'm not sure exactly what you mean . . .

Agreeing
- Yes, that's right.
- Right, yes, . . .
- Yes, . . .
- (Yes, and . . .)
- (Wouldn't you agree that . . .)
- (I agree that . . .)
- (I would agree with you that . . .)

Disagreeing
- Well, I wouldn't put it quite like that.
- It depends what you mean by . . .
- OK. But . . .
- But I think there's more to it than that . . .
- (but . . .)
- (Where I differ from your position is . . .)

3.2   Time needs to be allowed for preparation before the groups start their discussions. After the discussion, they need to reflect on their discussion techniques, rather than on the effectiveness of the arguments they presented. If you feel your class may have difficulty in objectively reflecting on their techniques, you may suggest that one member of the group acts as an observer/recorder who reports back to the group, but does not take part in the initial discussion.

3.3   Possible answers:
- So what you're saying is that poverty is the result of both the individual and the society.
- Let me just make sure – your point is that neither the individual nor society is solely responsible for poverty.
- Have I got this right – your view is that no one individual is solely responsible for his or her own wealth?
- If I understand you correctly, your argument is that society alone cannot be held responsible for the poverty found in many of the world's slums today.

3.4
- is your argument that . . .
- Just a minute, can I just get clear what you two are saying?
- Is your point that . . .
- In other words, . . .
- My point is that . . .
- So let me see if I've got this straight . . .

– We didn't really mean to say that . . . what we really meant to say was that . . .
– Yes, so . . .

4.1–4.2 When discussions go wrong, students often blame the teacher, as he or she is there to 'teach'. However, students need to be encouraged not to see themselves and others as passive pawns for the teacher to manipulate and put information into. Students need to be encouraged to take an active, responsible view of themselves as learners, in which the teacher acts as the facilitator who provides opportunities for learning. There is no way a teacher can guarantee someone will learn unless that person wants to learn. 'You can take a horse to the water, but you can't make it drink!'

In this conversation, the students blame the teacher and other students for the failure of the discussion. This is a positive first step, as some students may have blamed themselves either for a lack of language or a lack of self-confidence. However, the next step needs to be to consider action in which the learner takes positive steps to ensure that the discussion is a success.

For the 'dos' and 'don'ts', see the list in 4.2c.

The more practice students get in preparing and taking part in discussions, the more effective the discussions will become. If you feel your students need more practice using the language of discussion, as well as thinking (speaking) 'on their feet', then we suggest that other topics of interest be chosen for additional practice. It may also be helpful if different students act as observers, as it is often difficult to be objective in the heat of the moment.

UNIT **8** **Getting started on writing**

In this and the next unit, the aim is to introduce students to the fundamentals of academic writing – planning and writing an academic essay. This unit deals with the thinking and research that goes into the first draft. It should be noted that it has not been possible to cover the details of all the other main types of academic writing (e.g., dissertations, experimental reports – but see 10.4 – etc.). Rather, the academic essay has been used to illustrate the general principles (e.g., how to focus on a writing topic) which can be applied to other types of writing as the need arises.

1.1–1.3 There are no single correct answers; students are encouraged to assess their own strengths and weaknesses, in order both to build on the strengths and to develop the weaknesses.

1.1a Ensure the students understand what each of the skills involves first.

1.1b–d Make sure the instructions for doing these activities are clearly understood. With regard to **b**, it is likely that a good case can be made for regarding *all* the skills as important.

Section 2

Make sure that the students are clear about the concept of 'focus' as explained in the introduction to this section. (Check they know what a telescope is and how it works.)

2.1 More than one correct answer may be possible here – it depends on the reasons put forward. Also, it should be explained to the students that academic tutors may not always observe the finer distinctions, e.g., *outline* and *summarise* may not necessarily be distinguishable in practice. The main point is that students should consider as carefully as possible what the key words imply in terms of the basic slant required.

    1 d; 2 j; 3 o; 4 f; 5 l; 6 c; 7 a; 8 n; 9 i; 10 m; 11 c; 12 k; 13 h; 14 b; 15 g; 16 e.

2.2
1 What is meant by *working class*?
  What differences could I focus on?
  How are the groups alike?
  What difference(s) stand(s) out as most significant?
  What are the social, political, economic factors involved in calculating class?

2 What effects could be looked at: political; social; economic; ecological?
  What is the extent of the deforestation?
  What is/are the cause(s) behind deforestation?
  When did deforestation begin to occur?
  What was life and the economy like before deforestation?
  How dependent are the economies on money earned by deforestation?
  What are the economic alternatives to deforestation?
  What are the ecological problems resulting from deforestation?
3 What is meant by government; nation; deserve? How do you decide?
  What countries seem to have 'good' governments; 'bad' governments?
  What basis is behind these judgements?
  What happens when people try to change governments?
  How do I feel about this? What are my instincts and prejudices or bias?
  Can these be justified? How?
  What examples do I know of people who have tried to change
  governments and failed?
  Why did they fail?
4 Define *developing world*. Which countries are being referred to?
  Is the role of women in these countries always the same?
  How do they differ?
  Which women are being referred to – rich, educated, rural, . . . , and what
  percentage does each represent in that country?
  Is there *one* role that can describe most women?
  How are roles ascribed? What function do they fulfil?
  How do the roles of women compare to the roles of men?

2.3   These are merely suggestions, as it depends on how the paper is
focused. These positions are not necessarily our own, nor necessarily
accurate. They do, however, represent various ways the topics could begin to
be focused.
1 Position: There are three main differences – political, economic and
  sociological.
  – political
    – power
    – unions
    – support systems
    – women and minorities
    – voting and representatives
  – economic
    – earning power/wages
    – standard of living
    – cities vs rural areas
  – sociological differences
    – empowered
    – rights
    – social standing
2 Position: The long-term effects of deforestation will be devastating on S.E.
  Asian economies.
  – traditional survival systems gone
  – alternative sources of income undeveloped

- international trade and exchange lost
- arid and infertile land unable to provide food and raw materials for employment leading to widespread poverty, unemployment, and possibly starvation
- reduction in tourism resulting from climatic and scenic changes

3 Position: Nations seldom get the government they deserve.
- define nations as a group of people recognising a cultural identity – which may or may not be equivalent to a country
- unaggressive and undemanding peoples are often open prey to dictators (the Kurds until recently, for example)
- no political redress for nations, short of terrorism (the Palestinians in the 1950s)
- people lack money and arms to change the governments (the Chinese in the late 1980s)
- chance and wealth often determine the government, not rights or justice (USA for example)

4 Position: Women tend to take a backstage role in many developing countries.
- statistics of number of women heads of state, ministers, influential politicians, . . .
- no guaranteed rights, career structure, employment opportunities, etc., to reach the top except through family or marriage
  - China (Madam Zhao)
  - Pakistan (Benazir Bhutto)
  - Philippines (Imelda Marcos and Corazon Aquino)
- traditional role of women and how adapted to modern world, i.e., same but in a different guise
- responsibilities and role of women in the third world today (entertaining, press, positive image making, 'good deeds', . . .)

2.4
1 a; 2 a; 3 a; 4 a; 5 a; 6 a; 7 c; 8 b; 9 a; 10 b; 11 b and c; 12 a; 13 a and b; 14 a; 15 a; 16 a and c.

3.1   The intended order is as follows: 3, 5, 2, 1, 4, 6, 7. Other sequences are possible, but would need to be justified.

3.2   This is the beginning of a possible outline of the paper. b) refers to ideas from the reading passage. If students have difficulty, you may wish to write this outline on the blackboard.

I   What is meant by learning?
  A   The role of education is to provide the skills needed for tomorrow's world. (9)
II   Past thinking about how learners learn best
  A   Children used to have to memorise long passages. (3)
III   Present thinking about how learners learn best
  A   Learning involves the whole person. (4)
  B   Information needs to be understood to be useful. (5)
  C   Children learn best if they are contented and happy. (b)
  D   Child-centred (b)

IV What is rote learning?
    A Rote learning means memorising without necessarily understanding.
      (1)
V Why is rote learning unpopular among educationalists today?
    A The world is more complex, and people need to be flexible. (7)
    B Rote learning is boring. (10)
    C Produces negative attitudes towards schooling. (b)
VI Rote learning has a place in today's schools
    A People need to be able to recall information quickly. (2)
    B Education standards are declining, and children are able to recall
      fewer facts. (6)
    C Rote learning is easier to assess. (8)
    D Rote learning produces better exam results. (b)
VII Future role (b)
    A mixed (b)
    B need for more research (b)

3.2–3.3 Developing a focus or slant is difficult; magnifying it is even more difficult as it requires going into depth while maintaining sufficient breadth to cover the assigned topic. It is a difficult balancing act. The sequence information is presented in should support the focus while at the same time making it easy for the reader to follow.

3.4 Students may write on a topic of their choice. It is important that their ideas are arranged in an order that supports their position. If their order is unclear or unusual, ask them to explain/justify the order they have chosen, and perhaps to contrast it with more orthodox arrangements. Whatever order is chosen, students should be encouraged to examine their decisions critically.

4.1 The first one should be **b**, the last two should be **d**, followed by **c**: (b, —, —, —, —, d, c). However, there are four possible orders for the remaining part, depending on whether it is felt desirable to group ideas by issue (e.g., educational role of zoos) or side of the fence (pro- or anti-zoo), whether the educational or the conservation issue should come first, and whether the pro- or anti-zoo ideas should come first. The possibilities are thus:
1: e–a–f–g (educ. for, educ. against, conser. for, conser. against);
2: e–f–a–g (educ. for, conser. for, educ. against. conser. against);
3: a–e–g–f (educ. against, educ. for, conser. against, conser. for);
4: g–f–a–e (conser. against, conser. for, educ. against, educ. for).
    Since the evidence is pretty evenly balanced on both sides, we don't think it makes much difference which way it goes in this particular instance. However, there would be other cases where it would probably matter much more, e.g., if your intention was to argue strongly in favour of one side or another of an issue, then it would be best to put the points *against* your stance first (as otherwise your reader will not be paying attention but thinking of 'ah, buts'). Students could be asked to think of instances like this.

4.2

h   doesn't add anything substantial to ideas in first draft, so leave out
i   to come after **m**
j   to come at the end
k   *could* be added after **f** in Task 4.1, though does not add much to what already said, so not essential
l   irrelevant, therefore to be excluded
m   comes after **g** in Task 4.1
n   relevant on surface only: therefore omit

The full essay is as follows, using permutation **1** from Task 4.1. Possible linking words have been added for clarity.

Do zoos help or hinder the preservation of wildlife? There are a number of major arguments in both directions. In what follows, I shall first of all present each of them in turn. Then, in the light of these views, I will attempt to give my own answer to the question.

First of all, supporters of zoos argue that they have an important role in educating the public, millions of whom visit British zoos each year. Although television programmes about wildlife are available, there is no substitute for encountering real animals, they argue. The only way that most people can have first-hand experience of animals from around the world is by coming across them in zoos. Without this kind of contact, wildlife lacks reality for the ordinary person. It therefore becomes difficult or impossible to educate the public properly about wildlife: it is simply too remote from their experience. Such education is vital, however, if people are to become properly aware of their responsibilities for wildlife conservation. Thus, according to this view, zoos are seen to play an important indirect role in wildlife conservation, in terms of raising awareness about wildlife among the public in general.

On the other hand, opponents of zoos argue that much of what people see in zoos is undesirable. Captive animals are often kept in poor and inhumane conditions, zoo opponents say. In the worst zoos, animals are still displayed for the entertainment of the public. Where animals are placed in impoverished and unsuitable surroundings they often behave in abnormal or neurotic ways.

For example, it is common for polar bears constantly to pace up and down and twist their heads and circle over and over again. This behaviour is now recognised by scientists as a sign of stress and frustration. When people visit zoos where animals are acting in neurotic and abnormal ways, they are not being educated. Instead, opponents say, they are being given an inadequate picture of animal behaviour. A more precise and informative impression is available to the public through wildlife programmes on television. From this point of view, it could be argued that zoos actually have a negative effect on people's attitudes to wildlife.

Secondly, supporters of zoos point out that over the past twenty years zoos have developed programmes designed to help preserve endangered species. This involves breeding animals in captivity – in 'captive breeding programmes' – and then re-introducing them into their natural habitats to replenish the number living in the wild.

For example, the Arabian oryx (a kind of deer found in the deserts of Saudi Arabia and Jordan) were hunted by shooting parties until there were only about 30 left. In 1962, three oryx were taken to Phoenix Zoo, Arizona. By 1972, Arabian oryx had become extinct in the wild but had bred successfully in Phoenix and other zoos. In 1982, oryx were released back into the wild in Jordan.

Zoos co-operate with each other in order to ensure the success of their breeding programmes. Animals are passed from one zoo to another in order to prevent inbreeding – breeding from closely-related animals. If animals that are closely related to one another mate, there is a danger they will produce deformed offspring.

Opponents of zoos accept that some species have been saved from extinction by 'captive breeding programmes'. *However*, they also argue that this offers no solution to the worldwide conservation crisis. They say that the number of animals protected by zoos is tiny compared with the overall problem. It cost about £25 million to save the Arabian oryx from dying out; but could that amount be found for every species that is endangered? Zoo opponents say that zoos are not the answer because they are too costly. Habitat protection is the only solution.

Zoo opponents *also* argue that the existence of zoos may actively contribute to endangering certain species, rather than conserving them. There is a thriving trade in orang-utans, which come from Indonesia. They are generally sold in Singapore and other cities in the Far East to pet shops and East European zoos. For every orang-utan that arrives in a zoo, five are thought to die during capture and transportation, which adds to the decline of the species.

The value of zoo-breeding programmes is *also* questioned on the grounds that some species, such as the African elephant, do not reproduce well in captivity. Some zoo opponents fear that the result of breeding programmes may be new species of 'zoo animals' which are adapted to living in captivity, not in the wild. They say that the money spent each year on zoos around the world (about £250 million) would be better spent on protecting animals' natural habitats, such as the Tsavo Rhino Sanctuary in Kenya, where the black rhino has been brought back from the brink of extinction through careful management in the wild.

To sum up, there appear to be strong arguments both in favour of and against zoos. As we have seen, it can be argued that zoos may have a positive effect in terms of education and conservation. However, it can also be argued that this is clearly not always the case, and zoo opponents point out that viable alternatives exist, such as television programmes and the protection of natural habitats.

So, do zoos help or hinder the preservation of wildlife? The answer would appear to be both 'Yes' and 'No'. Some would say that this is inevitable. All zoos are a compromise. No matter how hard they may try to take into account the needs of their animals, they must always balance these with the expectations of the visiting public. It would thus appear difficult for display and conservation to go hand in hand.

Perhaps, *however*, there is an alternative. The zoo environment and the natural habitat of wildlife have traditionally been thought of as opposites. But it might be more productive to think of developing zoos so that the conditions in which the animals are kept resembled their natural habitats far more than tends to be the case nowadays. This would help to develop the potential of zoos for education and conservation. In other words, rather than abolishing zoos, the answer may be to change their nature. This can only help to make zoos a beneficial factor in wildlife conservation.

5.1   There are no set answers to the questions that they may ask, so make them suit your class's needs. We suggest a short paper of perhaps five or six short paragraphs, about 300 words at the most.

UNIT **9**   **Getting the writing right**

This unit is a continuation of Unit 8. The main aim is to get the students to develop an ability to edit their draft essays at the different levels necessary, from overall organisation down to the mechanics of grammar and vocabulary.

1.1
- Marco's writing: too opinionated; doesn't give any idea about how he will develop his writing.
- Silvana's writing: the best, as it states what will be shown and how this will be done. It outlines the organisation of the whole essay and the writer's attitude to the topic.

Note This amounts to a promise by the writer of what is coming later; this implies that either a firm plan has been drawn up or that the basic essay has already been drafted.
- Hiroko's writing: interesting but it doesn't give the reader any idea what her own position will be or how it will be developed; probably the weakest introduction.

As a further point, we suggest you encourage your students to try to avoid making the first sentence *This essay will be/is concerned with*, etc. Instead, suggest that they use a question or a quotation or some other device which starts the essay more indirectly. This is less predictable, and will therefore get the reader's attention better. Of course, they should then go on as straightforwardly as possible.

1.2a

cause/effect	comparison	contrast	addition	examples	conclusion	time
as	likewise	although	also	for	accordingly	as soon as
as a result	similarly	but	and	example	in brief	at the
because		besides	in	for	in short	same time
consequently		however	addition	instance	in	as long as
hence		nevertheless	moreover	in other	conclusion	at length
since		on the	too	words	on the whole	meanwhile
so		other		in effect	to sum up	secondly
thus		hand		in this		first of all
therefore		on the		case		finally
		contrary		in		
		otherwise		particular		
		while		specifically		
		in contrast				
		and yet				

48

1.2d

Those who oppose the legalisation of euthanasia do so for three main reasons. *(1) First*, they fear that it will increase the number of murders. They believe this is likely because it will be difficult to be sure in certain cases whether the cause of a person's death was their own wish or not. Someone wishing to murder an ill or elderly person will be able to make the death look like euthanasia. *(2) Thus*, from this point of view, euthanasia is likely to endanger lives.

The second main objection is medical. If euthanasia is permitted, some doctors argue that they would inevitably be the ones who were called on most often to carry it out. This would place an intolerable burden on them. It would *(3) also* mean that the patient would be able to make decisions about whether to live or not regardless of the doctor's judgement. Doctors would *(4) therefore* no longer be in a position to do whatever they thought was in the best interests of their patients.

The third reason usually put forward for opposing euthanasia is that it is against widely-held religious beliefs. According to this view, life is sacred, and no human being has the right to decide to take away life, even his or her own, or to help someone else to do so.

These objections are all seen as unreasonable by supporters of euthanasia, *(5) however*. They say that even if euthanasia made it easier to commit murder, there is no proof that this would automatically increase the number of murders. The opportunity to commit a murder does not of itself cause murder to take place. As regards the medical objections, proponents of euthanasia say that doctors are already called upon to make life or death judgements, as when, *(6) for example*, the decision is made to turn off the life-support machine of a patient in a coma. They *(7) also* argue that doctors do not have the right to make the ultimate decisions about a patient's care. *(8) Finally*, those in favour of euthanasia argue that human beings are seen by many religions as responsible for their own actions. It is up to the individual in the end to decide what his or her behaviour will be, and to accept the consequences. *(9) Thus*, from this point of view, deciding whether to end one's life or to help another to do so is a matter of individual responsibility.

1.3

1 Silvana does not state what she has shown, nor does she state her opinion/ conclusions.
2 Silvana introduces a new argument in the conclusion.
3 This is the best conclusion as it summarises her argument, states her conclusions, and indicates how these were arrived at.

2.1a   These are possible answers:

1 (*supporting details*) First, the legislative branch . . . Secondly, there is the . . . The judicial branch forms the third side . . .
2 (*reasons for a point of view*) One problem obviously concerns . . . Of course, another threat is to . . . However, there is another threat, often overlooked . . .
3 (*steps in a process*) The immediate effect of deforestation is an increase in . . . This leads to an increased dependence . . . However, the long-term effects are much more alarming, though no less direct . . .

4 (*practical examples/reasons for a point of view*) First look at development
aid and how it could be argued that it should increase self-reliance (*with
examples*) . . . Then, refute this theory by looking at examples where aid
ended in dependence.
5 (*reasons for a point of view/practical examples*) Look at children's daily
arithmetic needs which do not require calculators (*with examples*); then
look at arithmetic required to use the calculators (*with examples*).

2.2   The linking words that join the sentences into a cohesive paragraph are
in italics.

1 When it comes to the arts, there is a clear case for subsidy. The arts have
nothing to do with making money. They exist in order to express certain
essential truths about human beings by means of new kinds of poetry, music,
painting and so on. *However*, these new kinds of art may not be popular, *and
thus* there may be little support by the general public for them, *and so* artists
cannot rely on selling their work to provide them with an income. *In fact*,
history shows that many artists have not been properly appreciated while
they were alive. *For example*, Mozart, whose works are so popular
nowadays, lived close to poverty most of his life.
2 There are no grounds for subsidising the arts. The arts are not like food,
education or health, which are part of the basic necessities of life, and which
should *therefore* be subsidised if necessary. *On the contrary*, most of us live
our lives quite happily without paying any attention to the arts. They appeal
only to a small minority and are a luxury, rather than an essential.
Furthermore, those who value the arts can usually afford to pay the costs
involved. The large corporations that buy the paintings of artists such as Van
Gogh for millions of dollars *are a case in point*.

2.3   Somchart: 6; Alphonse: 5.
1 Somchart is more concerned with the true purpose of arts rather than
  simply their survival, which he doesn't mention.
2 This is another opinion, not a summary of either position.
3 This is an irrelevant detail.
4 This is an additional argument that Alphonse could have used, but didn't.

2.4
7, 14, 5, 3, 9, 13, 1, 11, 4, 12, 8, 10, 2, 6
The complete text should read as follows:

Alcohol is quick to act. It takes just twenty minutes (less on an empty
stomach) for it to pass into the bloodstream and all around the body,
including the brain. Its effect is to lessen control over muscles, slow down
reactions, make vision unclear and decrease awareness. And although its
action is rapid, the effects of alcohol wear off only slowly. It takes the body
an hour to eliminate a single unit of alcohol (equivalent to half a pint of
normal strength beer). Even sleeping for eight hours only removes the alcohol
from four pints of ordinary beer. Coffee may wake the drinker up slightly
but that is all. Nothing can remove alcohol from the blood, except time.
   How does drinking affect driving? As well as its bodily effects, drinking
gives drivers a strong (but false) sense of confidence, making it difficult for

them to judge how fit they are to drive. As a result, some drivers believe, wrongly, that they drive better after a few drinks. In fact, young and inexperienced drivers are unable to drive properly after drinking less than the legal limit of alcohol. Three or four units make such drivers three times more likely to have an accident than those who have drunk no alcohol. Thus psychologically as well as physically, and especially with young people, alcohol can have a serious effect on driving ability.

2.5   We would like to suggest that these are the qualities of a good paragraph:
– relevant overall framework of ideas in relation to the topic sentence
– ideas in a logical order
– correct use of logical connectors
– final sentence that paraphrases the paragraph as a whole
However, this list is not definitive, and other qualities could be added.

3.1   The symbols we suggest are listed in Appendix 6 on page 210 of the Student's Book.

It is commonly believed that scientists and artists have completely different ways of looking at the world – what C. P. Snow called *The Two Cultures* in his book with the same title. According to this view, the scientist relies for his discoveries on 'the scientific method', a careful process of objective experimentation and analysis. The artist, on the other hand, creates his works of art as a result of 'divine inspiration', a subjective leap of the imagination. I will argue that both of these views over-simplify the picture, and that the similarities between the ways that scientists and artists work are much greater than the differences.

3.2   The symbols can be found in Appendix 6 on page 210 of the Student's Book.

First of all, many important scientific discoveries have taken place by chance, rather than because of the scientific method. Diesel, the inventor of diesel fuel, is said to have seen the structure for the fuel in the pattern of raindrops on a window. The discovery of penicillin occurred when Fleming and his colleagues were actually working on a completely different problem. That he noticed the effect of the penicillin mould on bacteria was purely good luck. There are many other examples of similar events. Thus scientific discoveries cannot be said to occur only as a result of the scientific method.

3.3   The parts in italics could be omitted.

Secondly, there is plenty of evidence that not all great works of art are the result of sudden inspiration. *In whatever branch of the arts we look, things are similar.* In painting and music there are certain basic rules of composition which are usually followed. *The artist or the composer is not completely free.* Poems which appear to have been written effortlessly are in fact often the result of many careful, conscious rewritings. *Many poets constantly revise their poems.* For example, in a famous essay, Edgar Allan Poe describes the procedure he followed in composing the great poem 'The Raven'. *This is one* of his best-known poems. *Each verse contains the word 'nevermore'*. In the essay, he talks about how he gradually thought out the smallest details of each part, working methodically from beginning to end, all the time attempting to produce the appearance of inspiration. The finished poem appears very natural, but in fact was very carefully constructed. *The product was the result of a systematic working out of a plan.* In other words, we should be careful not to mistake the appearance of the finished artistic product with the process that leads to it. *Whatever the nature of the former,* the latter may be much closer to the methodical approach of the scientist than is usually realised.

3.4a   Students should be encouraged to ask their subject teachers what their policy on this matter is. They should try to get the subject teachers to provide them with concrete advice such as a style sheet, i.e., a set of examples of expressions which are acceptable and ones which should be avoided.

Clearly, more than one set of answers is possible here. The corrected passage *could* read:

As I have tried to show, there are good reasons for questioning the view that scientists and artists work in completely different ways. It is well known that chance can play a role in scientific discoveries. Similarly, a careful method of working can be an important part of producing a work of art. The real difference between scientists and artists may be not so much the way they work, but the materials they work with and the 'languages' they use to express their ideas. The scientist is mainly concerned with trying to understand the natural world, the artist with the world of the imagination. The scientist communicates with mathematics and facts, the artist through colours, shapes, sounds and fiction. But both are concerned with trying to discover and express truths. The search for truth in any area involves both science and art. The idea of the two cultures is therefore a myth.

3.5   Students should not feel they have to use the symbols we have introduced. What is more important is that they have a system of symbols that they can use efficiently. The corrected passage should read:

Patent law, which protects an invention from being copied, was originally devised in Europe in the fifteenth century in order to encourage innovation. Before this time, an inventor had no legal way of stopping other people from copying his or her inventions. It was therefore difficult for inventors to make money from their ideas. However, when patent law began, a much greater number of inventions began to come into existence.

Most of these inventions have been technological. This is because inventors can usually make more money from technological inventions. As a result, Europe and other parts of the West have become highly technological societies. However, this has reduced the level of creativity and innovation in non-technological areas. Inventors are less interested in non-technological inventions because there is less money to be made from them. Patent law needs to be changed to encourage social as well as technological innovation, such as better systems of education, new ways of looking after the sick and elderly, improvements in leisure-time opportunities, and so on. Unless this happens, there is a danger that technological inventions will lead only to further industrialisation, and the need for social developments will be neglected.

4.1a

1 Plagiarism is presenting someone else's ideas as your own.
2 Yes, but you must acknowledge the source of all ideas that you use.
3 Quotation marks are required when you use someone else's exact words, but not if you paraphrase or refer to ideas.
4 The date of publication.
5 Plagiarism can result in heavy penalties (possible failure or a requirement to resubmit or a downgrading of the mark being awarded).
6 Yes, but they must not copy other students' work, or try to pass off someone else's ideas as their own.
7 This is plagiarism, with a similar result.
8 In the same way, i.e., this is also plagiarism.

4.1b

1 There is no one correct paraphrase. Here are two possibilities:

Irish (1982) believes that job-seekers need to rid themselves of typical myths before they start looking for jobs.

Irish (1982) has developed a list of some tips to help people prepare for an interview.
2 According to Irish (1982), 'the smart job-seeker needs to rid herself of several standard myths about interviewing before . . . looking for a job' (my omission).

4.2

Faults	Problems
1 difficult to read	handwriting margins (not wide enough) spacing (not double-spaced)
2 no headings	hard to follow where the student is going
3 don't use appendices	waste time hard to follow main idea
4 improper use of diagrams	unclear what they refer to
5 too many and too long footnotes	lose track of the main idea
6 no useful information on the title page	bad impression easy to lose or mislay

The importance of headings (and sub-headings) in presenting written work clearly should be emphasised. This has not been the focus of any of the tasks for logistical reasons (i.e., the length of text necessary for an activity of this kind). However, good use of (sub-) headings is a vital aspect of 'signposting', and we suggest that this is given the attention it deserves in your feedback on the writing the students produce when carrying out some of the other tasks.

UNIT **10 Coping with research**

The aim of this unit is to enable students to understand and use some of the basic concepts and techniques involved in empirical research. This should also help them to interpret accurately empirical research data which they encounter in their reading. It is also hoped that the work will provide a positive foundation on which to base the students' own research and its presentation. Needless to say, however, this unit acts only as an introduction to the topic.

1.1

Jeffrey: Distance travelled for the purpose of shopping
– Difficulties: bias in sample, inconsistencies in time and place of interviews
Kate: Kinds of shops in town, and number of vacant premises
– Difficulties: imprecise definitions related to the purpose of the survey, problems in presentation

1.2   There is no set answer; students should discuss how they would use whatever methods they match to the topic. The answers below are merely suggestions. Students may wish to suggest research methods not listed.

1 *Sampling* Send out a questionnaire to all the postgraduate students at a university.
2 *Examining records* Look at the unemployment statistics and attempt to correlate these with other social and economic factors.
3 *Experiment* Put some computers in a classroom and observe any changes in writing. Compare these with a class not using computers.
4 *Observation* Visit a wealthy housing estate and count the number of houses with posters supporting the different parties.
5 *Sampling* Interview car salesmen.
6 *Observation* Watch children before and after they have been spanked and observe their behaviour, and continue the observation for several weeks, noting what happens each time the child is spanked.
Note We are not advocating children be spanked in the interest of science!

1.3

1 unrepresentative – time and place do not represent population of all shoppers in the city
2 unrepresentative – party members do not represent the population of voters of all parties
3 unrepresentative – the water in the district must include the water outside the town, and the water being sampled is not even representative of the water in the one river
4 unrepresentative – pre-school children do not represent the population of

children; in fact, pre-school children tend to have more colds than older children

5 unrepresentative – only a minority of people living in the city are likely to have come from farms, and the chances of interviewing these in this sample is small

6 representative – a true random sample

1.4   If the class has more than twenty students, the percentages for the class and for the sample should be nearly the same, though not identical, as there is always a margin of error. Students often feel that samples are unreliable, but as long as the sample is sufficiently large, this should not be the case. There are statistical formulae to test for reliability and the margin of error for different samples.

2.1   Please note the topic chosen here is deliberately light-hearted, in order to let the students concentrate on the research techniques in question, and to provide some relief from the more serious topics which are used in the rest of the unit. Such a topic also has the advantage of being neutral as far as the students' various subject specialisms are concerned.

1 Possible words: *like, breakfast, dinner, meat, supper, every day, tea, best, British, foreign, boring, old-fashioned, convenience food,* . . .

2 All of them. (Question 1, for example: What do you have for breakfast, What would you like for breakfast if you had lots of time and money, What do you usually eat when you have a choice, What do you like if your mother cooks it . . .)

3 Yes. (Question 1, for example: You may not like any of the food listed, or you may like all four together, or many other combinations, . . .)

4 One possible answer: British (English?) people eat a lot of boring, fried convenience foods as well as potatoes, and do not like exciting, healthy, foreign food. It is also assumed that the British have three meals: breakfast, lunch and supper, and that most people eat three meals a day.

5 No set answer. Possibly options like *none of these, other,* or leave the question open so that they can supply the answer. The questions themselves will not reveal the eating habits of the English (or British!), if that is the purpose. They may reinforce the stereotypes. Ideally, new questions should be written.

2.2   No set answers. Make sure questions relate directly to the topic, are precise and are unbiased. Questions should allow for a variety of answers, but also be capable of being tabulated. Language should not be ambiguous.

2.3   It is usually helpful to know what research has already been done, and what is already known about the subject generally, both in terms of theory and personal observation.

2.4b
1 Yes. (Just as if you have a pet, you are fond of all pets.)
2 Yes (as 1).
3 Yes. (This is put forth as the proof that links dislike of vicious dogs with an intolerance of other people's pets.)

4 Yes. (The dislike of cats spoiling gardens is also proof of an intolerance of *other* people's pets, and therefore it cannot be their cat – whether they do in fact own a cat is not known.)

5 Yes. (Same argument as in 4 except cats and pets are seen as equivalent.)

6 Yes. (Same argument as 4, 5 – if you are intolerant of dogs, you are intolerant of all pets.)

7 Yes (as 4, 5).

8 Yes. (As the people sampled wanted vicious dogs put down – implied because the dogs aren't controlled – and the general assumption of the paper is what is true for one kind of pet is true for all.)

9 Yes. (People must take responsibility for their pets is taken as proof that people are not fond of animals – hence most are not controlled – *in other words*, lines 9–10.)

10 Yes (as 9 *this position is supported* . . . , lines 10–11).

11 Yes (as 9 *therefore*, line 12).

2.4c We feel that none of these assumptions is logical, but students may disagree if they can justify their position.

2.4d

1 The English like their own pets.
   No support is given, as it is assumed that if you own a pet, you like it. This is not verified.

2 The English dislike other people's pets.
   No proof is offered of this, except that people do not like pets that are not under control. However, this does not mean that the English do not like pets generally, and it may be that what people do dislike is the pet's owner!

2.4e The population from which the sample was drawn believes that owners should be responsible for keeping their pets under control.

2.5 This is one of many possible systems.

	Man A	Man B	Woman A	Woman B
hours on Sat.				
favourite prog.				
improved?				
comments?				

3.1a–b Pie charts are good for visually illustrating one factor and comparing parts to the whole, but are poor at showing details and changes.

1 the whole class (100% of the class)

2 5

3 French

4 Chinese and Japanese

5 not known, as a pie chart can only illustrate one variable at a time

6 not known, as class size is not provided

3.1c

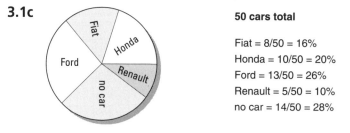

50 cars total

Fiat = 8/50 = 16%
Honda = 10/50 = 20%
Ford = 13/50 = 26%
Renault = 5/50 = 10%
no car = 14/50 = 28%

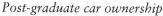

Post-graduate car ownership

3.2a–b Histograms are good for visually comparing various parts of a whole with each other, illustrating more than one variable in relation to each part.
1 25%
2 Japan or China (depending on interpretation of 'Fewest')
3 not known, as class size is not provided
4 20%
5 not known, as class size is not provided

3.2c

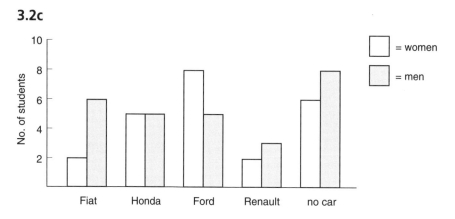

3.3a
  1 shoe size and age in years
  2 age
  3 age
  4 size
  5 3½
  6 4½ years
  7 no (see curve between 3 and 4)
  8 size of shoe
  9 number of children
10 4½
11 15
12 Three to five, assuming the child in diagram 4 is typical, as most of the children wear sizes 4, 4½ and 5, which corresponds roughly to three- to five-year-olds.

3.3b–c   Zubeda is showing improvement in Biology. Students need to make sure they have determined the correct dependent and independent variables, that the scale is reasonable and that the intervals are constant.

3.4
1 Actions – what is to be done.
2 Questions – decisions that must be made.
3 Which path to follow – where to go next.
4 Manufacture the product.
5 Do market research.
6 Find out if the product meets a need.
7 Investigate possible problems and causes.
8 When they feel they have no need for new products.

3.5   Guidelines for good diagrams should include:
1 simplify the information being conveyed
2 leave out unnecessary details in the drawings
3 label the parts clearly by writing the names in the margins and then drawing a simple line to each part
4 show movement with arrows
5 number the diagram and give it a title

3.6a
Average women: $25 + 29 + 20 + 19 + 27 + 29 = \dfrac{149}{6} = 24\frac{5}{6}$ years

Average men: $21 + 21 + 26 + 20 + 26 + 18 = \dfrac{132}{6} = 22$ years

Average of total: $\dfrac{281}{12} = 23\frac{5}{12}$

Conclusions: Women tend to read English at this university at a later age than men: the age range for women is 19 to 29, with a middle (median) age of 25 and an average (mean) age of 24⅚. This compares with a range of 18 to 26 for men, with a median age of 21 and a mean age of 22.

3.7
1 225 cm
2 300 cm
3 100 cm (mode)
4 Fertile range: 2 to 300 cm; infertile range: 3 to 290 cm.
5 Yes – a variety of genetic and environmental factors affects the growth of all living things.
6 Fertile, as the chances of growing a taller plant are greater, and the chances of obtaining a greater number of tall plants are also stronger.
7 No – although the chances are greater that the shorter plant would grow in the infertile soil, there is no certainty as the chances are there that for a variety of reasons, the taller plant may be in the poorer soil.

4.1
1 c; 2 d; 3 a; 4 e; 5 f; 6 b
One possible order of presentation: 1, 5, 4, 6, 3, 2

UNIT **11** **Getting to grips with assessment**

The aims of this unit are:
1 to look at various kinds of assessment in order to explore what is expected of students in each,
2 to explore different ways of preparing and taking exams successfully, and
3 to help students interpret and use assessment results effectively.

1.1   The answers are 1 C; 2 A; 3 B.

1.2a   There is no correct answer to this problem. Students need to discuss how it should be marked, e.g., are all the questions to be given the same number of marks or should some be weighted? Are spelling, neatness, and grammar important, and, if so, do they get marks even if the answer is wrong? How important is getting the answer right? And so on. Some points associated with each answer include:
1 spelling and neatness (answer is correct)
2 Grammar and spelling OK, but answer is only marginally correct; footnotes may not always occur at the bottom of the page. The question does not ask *where* footnotes are located, and this is irrelevant information – and information in a footnote may or may not be important. Footnotes a) provide information that is not directly relevant to the argument being presented, b) add backup information or references, or c) state the sources of the information.
3 *It might be an apple* is correct. However, adding *probably* to the answer suggests too strong a likelihood, and the addition of *it might not be* suggests that the writer isn't quite sure and is trying to cover all the options.
4 Possible questions given below. Questions of grammar and punctuation may also be addressed. The first two questions in the answer are really two ways of asking about the same reliability problem; the last question *why* may be interesting but goes beyond the scope of this research.
   a What is the population of men being studied? (e.g., country of origin, age of men, occupation, . . .)
   b What is meant by *bald*? e.g., losing hair, no hair on the top of the head, no hair at all, naturally bald or caused by disease or shaving, . . .
   c What is *an early age*?
   d How was the research conducted? (interviews, doctors' records, observation, . . .)
   e How does this conclusion compare with previous research?
   f How was the sample drawn and is it representative of the population of men?
   and so on . . .

5 Too long and complex an answer, ungrammatical, and misses the point of a straightforward answer. This answers the question *Why is it important to be able to read efficiently?*
6 States both important and unimportant points as if all of equal importance – thus indicating an inability to decide what is important. Numbering the answer would have helped limit the answer to the three main points asked for.

1.2b   There is a variety of advice that is relevant and acceptable – but the main point is that the knowledge is more important than grammar, spelling and punctuation, and that it is essential to answer the question as given clearly and concisely, as the teacher is not a mind reader.

1.3   It is important that this exercise is done in groups, as there is no single set of right answers. The aim is to explore ways of improving essays by looking at how essays can be approached and comparing these to the methods they use (both successfully and unsuccessfully).

1.4   Project work in the context of *Study Tasks in English* refers to any extended assignment done at home but used as part of the students' final assessment. There is no single set of answers, but we believe these are all advantages of project work for EFL students.

1.5   A summary exercise – no set answer. The aim is to make students more aware that different exams serve different purposes, that they are given for a variety of different reasons, and that they require different study strategies.

2.1   The purpose here is to encourage students to be in control of their learning even if they cannot control the actual assessment.

2.2   The aim here is to suggest ways to remember information. This book cannot train students in the actual use of some of the techniques. However, you may feel it would be useful for students to practise some of these techniques further by developing mnemonics for remembering all the planets, writing rhymes to remember unusual English words, and so on.

2.3   Robert has lots of problems, including studying in a noisy area, being disorganised, taking incomplete notes, listening to other students moaning, not studying regularly, not getting a good night's sleep, . . . There is no correct order of priority, as some students may feel that for them noise does not cause a problem, while for others making a timetable may seem to be a fruitless task.

2.4   Stress is a key factor in reducing student efficiency in exams. There are a variety of ways of reducing stress, and students should be encouraged to explore these. You may wish to practise some of the techniques as a class.

2.5   The aim for the day before an exam should be primarily practical – getting prepared. Study should be limited to a quick refresher and boosting confidence.

3.1   *Mr Jones*: most important is concise, relevant information, followed by neatness, correct spelling, grammar, and organisation.

Ms Smith: following instructions clearly and providing the information requested, followed by thinking clearly, logically and creatively.

3.2   Williem has many problems, especially not timing himself, pacing himself by other students, not looking ahead and not answering the easy questions first.

4.1   Musa was given specific advice about looking for underlying causes and considering different points of view. Mr Jackson explained about the marking system he used and offered extra assistance if desired. Teachers generally do not mind going over a student's exam with them, and teachers have been known to make mistakes. If a student is not happy after having visited their tutor, they should not be shy about asking for a second opinion or requesting the work be looked at by an external examiner as a last resort. *Note* A student should realise that a second marker may lower the mark; however, this should not discourage a legitimate complaint.

4.2   Most students are only familiar with the marking system(s) used in their own country. Students using *Study Tasks in English* may be attending colleges or universities in Britain, America, Australia, and so on (i.e., wherever English is the medium of instruction). They will need to develop an approach to coping with differences in marking systems, as it is not possible to describe the whole range within the context of this book. Coping with these differences includes finding out the criteria for marking, the range of marks being given, the percentages of students usually receiving different bands of marks, and so on. This awareness provides the means of assessing what the mark means in terms of the student's standing within the class as well as in terms of knowing how well he or she knew the material being tested.

4.3   Students often feel locked into an inappropriate course of study in which one failure follows another, creating stress. The failure may not be simply because the student is not up to the work; often it is because the student has lost interest or motivation but finds it difficult to face this fact and so simply 'hangs on'. Students should learn to use assessment as a means of determining their own long-term commitments. Students may need reminding that as their education continues, new avenues of interest will open up, while old ones may become more and more irrelevant. This relates back to 1.2.6, where students are asked to reflect about what they want to learn on a course and why.

UNIT **12** **Transportation in urban areas**

The aim of this and the following units is to practise using the study skills developed in the first eleven units. The tasks are designed so that the students listen, read, speak and write on a single theme in situations simulating study in higher education. Students are also expected to use skills involving critical thinking, questioning, evaluation, defining terms, conducting research, self-evaluation, and so on.

It is hoped that students will enjoy the topics, and will thus master study skills through actual study, with built-in self-assessment to highlight the study skills being used. We have tried to select a range of topics which we hope will be seen as of interest to students from a wide range of disciplines. Obviously, however, in doing the work of these units, students will have to be prepared to engage in study of topics which may not be central to their main specialism. If you find the students are resistant to this idea, we suggest that you discuss the problem with them. Hopefully, a consensus will emerge concerning the importance of being open-minded and of taking a broad view of what is relevant in a study and training situation. It should also be pointed out that none of the work involves the students in a specialised knowledge of the topic.

The aim of Unit 12 is to use the study skills acquired in *Study Tasks in English* in connection with the topic of transportation in urban areas. If students have an interest in some aspect of this topic which is not focused on directly in the unit, they can use the project-work element (see Task 1.2) as an opportunity to develop their special interest.

1.1–1.3 This section is meant as an introduction to the topic of transport. The project is a key element of the unit, and time must be given for students to work on their projects throughout their work on the remaining parts of the unit. Try to encourage students to think critically and logically about their project. The topic they choose may involve reading local newspapers, interviewing local people, or doing field research where, for example, they study traffic conditions outside class time. The topics listed are only suggestions. Students should write up their findings in order to practise their writing, organisational and critical thinking skills. They should also present the results of their project to the class, and Task 1.3 is intended to provide some guidance in this. You may wish to set a time limit for the presentation.

2.1–2.4 Ensure the students have taken adequate notes in Task 2.1 before going on. The main points in the talk are as follows:
- in next century, there will be an abandonment of the main 'solutions' to the problems of urban transport attempted in the second part of 20th century, viz.: highway building and mass rapid transit systems;

– instead, there will be a greater focus on:
- – management of transportation demand
- – attempting a 'package' of solutions, vs. a single, grand design
- – a systemic approach (i.e., seeing transportation in its wider socio-economic context)

3.1

1 Heavy traffic congestion on the roads around the university combined with excessive traffic speed endangering pedestrians and other car users.
2 Raise the speed limit to 30 m.p.h. except at a few particularly dangerous spots.
3 It might, but, more likely, it may simply legalise the existing problem without either easing congestion or making the areas safer.

3.2

1 *Position A*: There is a need for speed bumps on Marsh Road. However, not enough information has been provided in this letter to know if there is a significant traffic problem in the area. Nevertheless, the position is clear and to the point.
2 *Position B*: There is no need for speed bumps. However, the need for traffic control in this area is not disputed, so it must be assumed that the problem that Mr Davidson outlined in some previous letter does in fact exist. The dispute seems to centre on the method of solving the problem. However, no action has been taken for reasons that are unclear or unknown.
3 *Position C*: It is wrong to use methods of traffic control that are disliked by, or inconvenient to, drivers, especially as these may increase their reckless driving. Therefore, speed bumps are not recommended; rumble strips may be an alternative as these do not cause as much inconvenience, nor do they slow the traffic down to the same extent. Better still, educate children not to run into the road. Safety is really the pedestrian's responsibility, at least until someone is killed.

4.1a   These answers are suggestions only:
A1 Using the present infrastructure more efficiently can help alleviate the worst aspects of existing problems. (Examples include one-way systems and traffic light timing – these are not included in the article.)
A2 There are at least four ways to alter working times to relieve traffic congestion.
A3 The major benefits of car usage have gone to middle- and upper-income whites (with a widespread distance between home and work) while the negative impacts of the motor car have fallen on the minority, inner-city neighbourhoods.
A4 Lower-income families tend to suffer most from the most important source of urban pollution (air and noise), the motor car.
A5 Mass transit differs from the use of highways in that highway use is largely funded by the users whereas mass transport is largely funded by non-user taxes, as it is designed to reduce the negative impacts of the car.
A6 People are turning to past forms of transport, rather than new alternatives, to solve today's traffic problems.

B Privatised industries are usually monopolies whose pricing and services are tightly controlled. This may adversely affect their efficiency, and make them unsound investments.

C Build a mass-transit system, subsidised by the tax-payer, rather than building more roads, subsidised by tax-payers as well. Roads simply increase the problems.

4.2

1 Flexible work hours – where employees choose their own work schedule.
2 Electric streetcar.
3 The poor, minorities, and the unemployed.
4 The non-user tax-payer.
5 A positive image.
6 No, it may be a controlled monopoly under private rather than state ownership.

UNIT 13 Crime in the modern world

The aims of this unit are similar to those of the previous one.

1.1–1.2 Dr Hudson's main point is that although the definition of a criminal might seem straightforward at first sight, i.e., someone who breaks the law, in reality the matter is more complex than that. We do not always think of someone who breaks the law as a criminal, and, on the other hand, some people are thought of as criminals even though they have not broken the law. The main point is that it is really our concept of what is criminal, rather than that of the law, that often colours our judgement. Such concepts may vary politically, in terms of how we see the results, by gender, etc.

1 She says it really depends on your point of view, since it is clearly not just someone who breaks the law (although it may be such a person).

2.1

A Dr Carey claims the riots were rooted in social deprivation, linked to poverty, poor housing, illiteracy; the government claims the riots were pre-planned criminal activities, and that the church has a role to play in tackling the spiritual malaise in society.

B The role of schools is to prepare pupils for their future citizenship. Schools cannot right society's wrongs; they can, however, provide the education for a satisfying future life.

C Liberal policies that seek to understand and rehabilitate the criminal actually increase the number of criminals and make problems worse.

D Low self-esteem (i.e., image of one's own worth) associated with the discrepancy between the life many people would like (as seen in the media, for example) and the life they actually follow, causes people to turn to crime. To prevent crime, society must either provide the possibility of obtaining the desired life-style or change the images and class relations.

E One of the few means available for poor women in Nigeria to obtain urgently needed money is smuggling. These women face prison in both the UK and in Nigeria when they return. The numbers are increasing and the intended deterrent effect of harsh punishments does not seem to be working.

2.2

1 Tyneside.
2 In 1785 (about 200 years ago).
3 Chester, at a meeting of the Anglican Secondary School Heads.
4 Liberals – people seeking to understand criminals and what makes them criminals (seen by the author as people not interested in understanding the victims of crime).

5 Prison.
6 Six years.
7 Cookham Wood Prison, in Kent.
8 Decree 33.

3.1–3.4   There is no set answer for this seminar. Learners should be encouraged to prepare their arguments logically and critically. You may need to warn students about 'pat' answers, and methods that will solve all crimes. Learners need to be encouraged to define their terms, consider a variety of possibilities, and reflect on the consequences of the choices they make.
Note   In 'Crimewatch' crimes are constructed so that viewers can help to solve them. 'Scotland Yard' is the headquarters of the Metropolitan Police in London.

4.1–4.2   The skills needed for this project are similar to those needed in the previous unit. Students should try to choose a topic which requires different skills, if possible. For example, if they conducted an interview for the first project, this time they may wish to choose a topic requiring a greater use of reading. However, the choice should ultimately be left to the learners.

UNIT 14 Communication and the media

1.1–1.4   This is a simulation of a part of an initial lecture in a course on communication and the media.
Course aims:
– to understand how the media shape our picture of the world
– to evaluate critically the picture of the world presented by the media
Definition of terms:
– *communication*: the messages, images, ideas, and attitudes conveyed by the media
– *media*: the main means of mass communication in the modern world, i.e., newspapers, TV etc.

2.1 Text A   Note that the first excerpt was written by Orwell in 1942, and therefore refers to the political context of that time.

2.1 Text B   The earlier part of this excerpt talks about how the term *the economy* (vs. *economy*) emerged in the first half of this century, the change implying a shift away from a view of economics as something to do solely with natural law to a view of economics as something susceptible to government policy. Please note, however, that the students do not require any specialised knowledge of economics (or linguistics) to get the main point of the text (which is the way that metaphors used to describe concepts can change our view of the concepts and/or say something about how we view the concepts).

3.1a   The gist of each of the articles is as follows:
A Comparisons in advertisements are sometimes misleading because they appear to be comparing like with like when in fact this may not be the case. The 'meaning' of words being used in the comparison may not have changed, but the reference may have.
B Advertisements often mention a problem in everyday life, but then, rather than addressing it at its root, suggest instead a short-term fix, in the interests of selling the particular product being advertised.
C Television advertisements are capable of deceiving because they contain both sound and pictures and occur too fleetingly to be studied carefully. The mixture of channels means that one of the channels can be used to confuse or contradict the message in the other one. The speed factor makes it difficult to notice such techniques. Furthermore, although advertisers are usually careful not to make false claims directly, they may do so by implication. This is still dishonest, since it is known that viewers generally fail to notice this.

3.2a

1 In the example mentioned in the passage, although the name of the car did not change over the years, its specifications did. Thus, the name of the car still referred to the same basic model as the years went by, but significant features of the car (e.g., engine size) were altered.

2 In order to provide a reason for buying hair conditioner.

3 It is used as a way of creating the impression that an artificial habit created by the world of advertising is to be taken for granted as perfectly natural, and thus to lower resistance to further 'innovations' of this kind in advertisements.

4 Instead of getting at the root of a problem, it is addressed at its most immediate level only.

5 Because many products cannot be 'sold' adequately on the basis of their visual appeal alone.

6 We tend to focus predominantly on one or the other.

7 Because they are confused by confused or conflicting messages in the two channels, and because advertisements on TV do not last long enough to be checked carefully.

8 What an advertisement asserts is said directly and obviously; what it conversationally implicates is implied indirectly, and depends on viewers drawing their own, further conclusions.

9 Because the way people actually perceive advertisements is how they really understand them. The implication of this view is that it is dishonest and therefore undesirable to behave as if viewers were more discerning than they really are.

10 The author says 'it has been established experimentally that people tend to recall pragmatic inferences of sentences with as much or more frequency than they recall what was directly asserted.' He gives no details of the experimental conditions, and, in any case, his words are *tend* and *as much or more frequency*. Thus all that can be said is that experiments seem to show that people may behave in this way.

UNIT **15 Study in an academic context**

The aim of this unit is to revise several of the main points presented in *Study Tasks in English* and to encourage the learners to look back for a final time in order to both assess how much they have achieved and to consider ways of continuing to polish their study skills.

1.1–1.4 Many universities have initiation programmes where students are able to get study advice when they need it. This is simply one example.

1.2
1   . . . that he is ultimately responsible for his own learning.
2   . . . that he should talk to his tutors as soon as possible, and as soon as he thinks he is getting behind.
3   Ali's himself.
4   Various kinds – ask your tutor – librarians, leaflets, the EFL Centre, and so on.
5   EFL-related problems, like keeping up with the reading.
6–8 These are discussion questions with no single set of correct answers.

2.1
1 It doesn't take into account differences between learners.
2 Students should get to know their own natural approach to study and then find ways to make it work more effectively.
3 *Possible suggestions*:
   Neo: set periods for work and make a book list
   Bingo: set realistic targets and more purposeful study – less trying to cover everything
   Ricky-Tic: become more flexible, with less tunnel vision and to enjoy college more
   Cherry: become more ambitious and confident
4 No set answer.
5 Time to understand what's expected of the student and for the student to define their own objectives.
6 Study involves the whole person, and not just the academic study part; your physical and emotional set affect your attitudes and how you perceive study.
7 No set answer.

2.2   Any topic on study can become a project. Students should be encouraged to think deeply and critically about the aspect they choose, do some research on it (either through interviews and observation or through reading), and produce some conclusions that they can present to the class.

3.1–3.3   Managing time at universities and colleges of higher education can be difficult for students used to time being managed for them by parents and teachers. In further education, there are many demands on time – academic, personal and social. There are no set answers, but students should be aware of the pressures and discuss how they might be able to reach some balance. Part of the aim of this exercise is developing seminar, reading and note-taking skills. Students should have time to reflect on these matters.

4.1–4.2   Learning is an on-going process, and revision is an integral part of this process. One purpose of an exam is to help assess how much learning has taken place. How is the amount of study time for an exam measured: since the course began? A month before an exam? The week of the exam? The night before? Or what? Often students who appear to study less have been studying regularly over a long period of time, and whether the total time spent is greater is hard to determine. However, quality of time is more important than quantity. Students need to develop strategies for ensuring quality time. These include making sure the study is purposeful, relevant, understood, and so on.

UNIT 2, TASK 2.3

STEPHEN: Right, let's get down to work. How should we begin?

ALISON: Well, why don't we each say what we found out? I can take notes if you like.

STEPHEN: OK. Well, I've got a plan of the present school playgrounds. Over here there's a fairly large playing field for the older children to play football on. However, the younger children have only these areas around the school, about half of which are grass and the rest is paved. There isn't any play equipment for the children. This area on the right is so full of weeds that the children aren't allowed to use it.

ALISON: Right – but at least it looks like there won't be a problem of access between the school and those areas – there are plenty of doorways. On the other hand, though, noise might be a problem if we put playing equipment near the building.

STEPHEN: There are 350 children in the school, so noise must be a real problem all the time! Right, now what else have we got? Ah, yes, when I talked to the teachers they said the main problems for them were mud on wet days and keeping an eye on the children while they are playing to make sure they are OK.

ALISON: Right. I also spoke to the head teacher. Let me see . . . ah, yes, she's concerned about safety when the school is closed. Some of the children come and play but there's no one around to look after them.

STEPHEN: OK. Now, are there any other factors that you think we should consider?

ALISON: I took a look at the present play area and I noticed the pavement is very uneven and cracked – it's not safe at all. I also got the impression that vandalism is a problem.

STEPHEN: Yes, I've heard that there's a lot of vandalism in the area. Anything that isn't fixed or is expensive will probably be stolen. All the teachers park their cars at the front, to keep them safe.

ALISON: OK. Um, I also found out something about the kind of children there are in the school. There are several that are handicapped. Then there are about 50 children under five, and there are – let me see – ah, yes, 135 children between five and seven. They all use the play areas at the same time – the teachers try to keep them separate. There are (*pause*) four – yes, that's it – four teachers on duty each playtime, but none after school.

STEPHEN: Right . . . oh, by the way, something else I found out was that there should be enough money to do whatever we want. They're going to be able to get young people on job training to do a lot of the manual work, so that'll cut down on the expense a lot.

ALISON: Well, I think we've got enough details now to be getting on. Should we try sketching out a plan?

STEPHEN: OK, right. Well, I've been thinking about that field of weeds. It's near (*fade out*)

UNIT 3, TASK 1.3

PIERRE: Well, this essay shouldn't be too difficult – we already know what started the First World War – the shooting of Archduke Ferdinand by Gavrilo Princip. All we have to do is work out why Princip shot him.

JOE: Yes, and we know that he shot the Archduke because the Serbians and the Austrians hated each other. Princip was a fanatical Serbian nationalist and the Archduke was a powerful Austrian and heir to the throne.

PIERRE: And the reason the Serbians and the Austrians hated each other was because Serbia was a colony of Austria and wanted independence like most colonies want. That means that the war was really caused by colonial feelings and policies. I also happen to know already that Austria declared war on the Serbians when it couldn't get them to do what it wanted. So I think we need to find out how Serbia became a colony of Austria to understand the cause of the war.

MARGARET: Wait a minute. I've been listening to you both, but I think we should look at why this particular incident caused the war, not why he was shot. I've read a lot about the treaties that Russia, England, France and other countries had made with each other. These treaties meant that if almost anything happened in Europe, everyone would be drawn in. I personally feel that these treaties are the underlying cause of the war and I intend to look at them in great detail.

MICHAEL: But you can't stop with the treaties. I think we have to go on to ask why the countries decided to make the treaties. It's always seemed to me that the reason for those treaties was to justify and protect huge investments in the military – so we need to look into how and why the military became so strong. After all, without a military build-up, there can't be a war.

JOE: I think everything we've mentioned may be important, but I still think we need to look further. If you ask why – why the treaties, why the military build-up, why colonies, and so on, you will find it simply boils down to money – greedy capitalists wanting to make more money, as they did in fact do. I think I'll write my essay on 'World War I – the result of greed'.

MICHAEL: Slow down! I think you have the wrong end of the stick . . . (*fade out*)

UNIT 3, TASK 3.4

JAMES: Let's see how our mice have been getting on with that drug we injected them with yesterday.

JOAN: Right. – Oh dear, I'm afraid we'd better stop trying this one out.

JAMES: Why?

JOAN: They're all dead.

JAMES: Oh dear! What a waste – you know, I really wonder if it's right, carrying out these experiments with animals.

JOAN: I know what you mean. I don't like being responsible for animals dying either. But I don't think it's a waste. They didn't die for nothing, did they? We now know more than we did before about the effects of that medicine.

JAMES: Yes, but I don't think there's anything more important than life. What's the point of trying to discover new medicines if you end up harming or killing animals in the process? Isn't their right to life just as important as ours?

JOAN: Oh, I agree completely that other animals have a right to life. But I see these experiments as the lesser of two evils.

JAMES: What do you mean?

JOAN: Well, what I mean is that although you might kill some animals like mice or rats in the process, in the end you might discover a new kind of medicine that will help to save human lives.

JAMES: But that assumes that the lives of human beings are more important than the lives of other kinds of animals.

JOAN: I agree that all life should be protected as far as possible. But the world isn't always as simple as that. If you have to make a choice between perhaps saving human lives and running the risk of destroying those of other animals, what do you do?

JAMES: I wonder if there isn't a way of avoiding having to make that kind of choice in the first place.

JOAN: Well, put it like this. Would it have been better, for example, if Jenner hadn't tried out his smallpox vaccine on cows first of all? What would have happened? Would it have been better if humans had been used for the trials right from the beginning instead? We all know it works now, but that couldn't have been known then. What would have been better if it hadn't worked – a dead person or a dead cow? Or would it have been better if Jenner hadn't been allowed to experiment at all? If we had no smallpox vaccine as a result?

JAMES: I still wish we didn't have to make those kinds of choices in the first place.

JOAN: Yes, I agree – that's the real problem.

UNIT 4, TASK 1.6

JOHN: Hello, Mary. Fancy meeting you here!

MARY: Hi, John. Yes, I'm here again . . . and there always seems to be a queue. I'm writing a report for my Psychology class. How about you?

JOHN: I'm still working on my essay for Environmental Science. I need to check a reference.

MARY: You know, when I first started doing my report I was frightened to use these computer catalogues. I was sure something would go wrong.

JOHN: But they're so useful. You can see at a glance what books you need and if they're checked out or not.

MARY: I know that now, but at the beginning I really missed the card catalogues. But anyway I still have the same problem as I used to have – knowing what to look up!

JOHN: Yes, I agree there – it's the same for me. Last week I must have wasted two hours looking for information on a topic I was working on.

MARY: Really? What was the topic?

JOHN: It was about the effect of smoking by parents on their children's sleep. I looked up sleeping, child psychology, child development, problems in social work, children's medical problems, delinquency, and I can't remember what else. In the end, I had to go back and ask my tutor for help.

MARY: You know, I took a study skills class because I thought it would help me locate information, and all I learned was how to read the cards, which wasn't much help! My real problem is knowing what card to look up.

JOHN: Yes, and that takes thinking! Pity the computer can't do that for us.

MARY: Maybe it will some day. Oh, look – there's a free computer now.

JOHN: Thanks – and good luck! See you!

MARY: Yes, thanks. See you!

UNIT 5, TASK 3.2

1 There are many types of motivation that affect our everyday behaviour. However, three kinds which are often discussed are, first, the need for achievement; second, the need for affiliation; and third, the need for power. Let me just explain a little about each of them.

The first one, the need for achievement, is the desire we feel to succeed, especially to reach a target we have set for ourselves.

The second one – the need for affiliation – is our desire to belong, to have friends, to be a member of a group with similar ideas to our own, and so on.

The third is need for power. This is the need we have to have control over or to influence other people . . .

2 There are many different makes of personal computers in the world nowadays, but they are all operated in a similar way.

First of all, the machine has to be switched on and 'booted' – that is, the program that runs the basic functions of the computer, such as reading and writing to disks, has to be loaded. Depending on the machine, this program is loaded automatically from the hard disk or is run by inserting a special floppy disk into one of the disk drives.

Once the machine has been booted, you have to load the program you want to use. This might be a word-processing program for writing, or a spreadsheet for doing financial calculations, or a database for keeping records – the possibilities are almost endless. However, the program of your choice will have to be either selected from those stored in the computer on the hard disk, or loaded into it from a floppy via the disk drive.

Usually, you enter data into the computer program by typing it in at the keyboard. When this has been done, the result can be printed out or stored. If you wish to store it, however, it must be saved on a disk. If you switch the computer off without doing this, all your work will be lost!

If the computer is connected to a network – that is, if it is linked electronically to another computer, either directly or by a connection such as a telephone line – then it is also possible for the data that you have entered in your computer to be transferred via the network to any of the other computers that are linked to the same network. With some computers it is even possible to send a fax copy of your data directly from the computer itself . . .

3 There are two main theories about why people work. The first one, known as 'Theory X', assumes people only work because they *have* to. The other one, 'Theory Y', assumes people work because they *want* to.

Managers who adopt the Theory X view believe that most people really do not like working. They also believe that most people prefer to be told what to do, rather than having to think for themselves. They think that most people are not creative or good at problem solving, and they are only interested in working in order to meet their most basic needs. As a consequence, they feel most people have to be closely controlled and forced to meet the aims of the organisation they are working for.

On the other hand, managers who believe in Theory Y see work as being as natural as play, if the right conditions are provided. They believe that being able to have control over one's work is usually essential, and that the ability to solve problems is something most people are capable of. They see people as being interested in working not just for basic needs, but also because work helps them to feel good about themselves and to fulfil their potential. They therefore also believe that people can manage their work for themselves if they are led properly . . .

4 The process of successful population control is dramatically illustrated by the case of Thailand. In 1969 Thailand had a rapidly growing population. Women had, on average, 6.5 children. Fewer than one in six married women between the ages of 15 and 44 used any form of contraception. Family-planning organisations reported a large demand for family planning which was not being met. Population growth had begun to affect people's standard of living.

In 1970 the Thai government started a nationwide family-planning programme in an attempt to slow the growth rate of the population and improve the economy. It made contraception freely available and extended services into remote rural areas. It trained non-specialists to provide contraceptives. In 1980 the government ran a mass-media campaign to encourage family planning.

Within a space of twenty years the proportion of people using contraception has dramatically increased, from 14.7% to 68%. In 1990, the number of children per woman had fallen to 2.2. Because of the earlier 'baby boom', the population has still doubled to 55.7 million, but without the family-planning programme the figure would have been about 67 million. Living standards have gone up . . .

5 Let us look at some of the characteristics of the world's main religions.

First of all, *Buddhism*. Buddhism was founded about 2,500 years ago by Prince Siddharta Gautama who lived from about 563 to 483 BC in north-east

India. He was known as Buddha, a Sanskrit title meaning 'the Awakened One'. Its main writings are contained in a number of sacred books called the Pali Canon (Pali is the Indian language in which they are written), and in a vast collection of Sanskrit, Tibetan and Chinese sacred texts. There are now some 256 million believers, mainly in Southeast Asia and the Far East.

Next, *Christianity*. This was founded about 2,000 years ago by Jesus Christ, who lived from about 7 BC to AD 30. Its writings are contained in the Bible. There are now about 1,200 million believers in the world – including some 806 million Roman Catholics, 343 million Protestants and 74 million members of the Eastern Orthodox Church.

Let's move on to *Confucianism*. Confucianism was founded about 2,500 years ago by the philosopher Kong Zi, known by the Latin name Confucius, who lived from about 551 to 479 BC. His teachings are contained in what are now called the Analects, from the Greek word *analekta*, meaning 'a collection of facts and sayings'. There are now about 275 million believers, mainly in China and Taiwan.

Hinduism. Hinduism is the European name for the Santana Dharma, 'the Eternal Law'. The earliest Hindu text – the Rig Veda – dates from before 1000 BC. But the best-known texts are the Upanishads, Brahmanas and Puranas, collectively called the Veda, or 'Knowledge'. The most popular text is the *Bhagavad Gita*. There are now about 500 million believers in India and in Indian communities throughout the world.

Islam. Islam was founded about 1,400 years ago by the prophet Mohamed, who lived from about AD 570 to 632. Its holy scripture is the Koran. There are now about 1,100 million believers throughout the world . . .

UNIT 5, TASK 3.3

What can be done to reduce the dangers of global warming?

Well, it will obviously help if we cut down on the amount of carbon dioxide going into the atmosphere. It also makes sense for a lot more trees to be planted.

Both of these things are possible to do and will actually help national economies. One of the main ways a lot of the extra carbon dioxide gets into the atmosphere is by burning fossil fuels – like coal and so on. But a lot of this energy is actually wasted. Some of the fuel isn't burned properly, some of the heat produced is lost, some of the energy is used wastefully by lights being left on unnecessarily and so on. If we insulated and managed buildings properly, if we stopped using cars so much and had more efficient public transport systems instead, if the heat that is wasted in power stations was used to heat greenhouses and homes, if we burned coal so that we extracted more energy from it – if nations did all these things, they would not only cut down a great deal on the amount of carbon dioxide they produce, they would also save huge sums of money!

Tree planting has other benefits as well. About 25% of the carbon dioxide produced by people comes from clearing and burning forests. However, growing trees soak up carbon dioxide. If we stopped destroying forests and started to plant new ones the trees would help absorb greenhouse gases. But trees are also very useful as sources of building materials, fibres and medicines. They also hold soil in place, shelter wildlife, and increase rainfall. In other words, they not only help to reduce the greenhouse effect: they also make sound economic sense.

However, I should point out that in reality the picture is more complicated than this, of course. The way we use energy is not shared out on an equal basis throughout the world. The rich nations use about 70% of it, while the developing nations use the other 30%. This means that the 'greenhouse effect' – that is, the warming up of the atmosphere because of too much carbon dioxide – is a problem created by the rich nations. They now have to try to persuade the developing countries not to start increasing their use of energy. This will be difficult politically, because developing countries cannot raise the living standards of their people without using more energy. For example, if China carries out its plans to use more coal in the next 35 years, it will increase by about 50% the amount of carbon dioxide being released into the atmosphere at the moment.

There is another political problem. The countries of South America, Africa and South-east Asia are being asked to protect their rain forests. But the countries that are asking them to do so are the rich ones which cut down almost all their own wild forests centuries ago!

Something else we also need to remember is that the world's population is not standing still. In 1800 there were one billion people on earth; by 1940, the total was 2.5 billion. Now there are more than five billion. Before the end of the 1990s, there will be six billion. Every year there are another 92 million people in the world. They will need food, housing, transport, communications, education, hospitals and jobs. All these things require energy. They will need land, and this will mean more cutting down of more trees.

A real solution to the problem of global warming is therefore very difficult and complex. It requires the nations of the world to co-operate together in a way they haven't ever done so far. But the question they need to consider is no longer what is good for individual nations, but what is good for our planet as a whole.

UNIT 5, TASK 4.4

1 Nowadays, by far the most common technique for attempting to improve the way that students learn is to give them *training* in the skills they need. However, there are good reasons for questioning whether training is always the best way to do this. In the first place, it assumes that we know what study skills consist of. But do we?

Let us take the skill of note-making as an example. What does effective note-taking actually consist of? We might think the answer obvious. Not so. If we were to ask a roomful of successful academics to take notes from a lecture and then examine what they had done, we would find that they had all done something rather different, and that some people would have taken no notes at all. I am not merely guessing when I say this. I have used this as a demonstration on several occasions. The same is true of practically any aspect of study activity. Successful learners do different things and different techniques suit different people.

Moreover, even if we were to find one form of notes cropping up frequently, this would not be a good enough reason to train our students to take notes in this way. This is because although it is possible to observe what a note-taker is writing down – the layout, use of abbreviations and so on – it is extremely difficult to know about the mental processes of selection of subject matter, and the ways in which it is transformed and organised, which determine *why* particular items are written down. So, two sets of notes which look the same on the surface could have been produced by entirely different processes, for entirely different reasons, and with completely different learning outcomes. Training students in only the outward form notes should take is therefore not very helpful to them.

I am not arguing that we should not train students to take notes. What I am saying is that if we train students in a *generalised* way, without regard to the individual student, or the particular course he or she is taking, or the demands of the assessment system, and so on, then it is not very likely that we will have a positive effect. We do not, in general, know what the necessary skills are, and it seems unlikely that any exist.

2 So far, I have talked about two of the main dimensions of learning how to learn – needs, and learning styles. I now come to the third dimension of learning how to learn, and this is 'training' – the deliberate effort to help people become better at learning and more successful in the educational arena. Unfortunately, the term 'training' is sometimes thought of rather negatively. Nevertheless, it is very useful in understanding the learning-how-to-learn concept and in communicating about the process of helping people to acquire skill in learning and knowledge about education.

Those of you who put the information in this talk to work, the instructors who provide memory improvement exercises for students, the consultants conducting a study skills workshop – all three are involved in training, or have temporarily put on the training hat. Training can be designed to meet broad needs and competencies. It can pursue a global goal, like understanding the learning-how-to-learn concept itself, with its implications for self-directed, collaborative and institutional learning. It can also deal with such a highly specific matter as how to prepare correspondence study assignments or how to write a learning contract. Training can be built into ongoing instructional situations or stand as a separate event, say as a discussion skills workshop or a course in speed reading.

Training can last ten minutes or two weeks. Like almost any teaching–learning transaction, it can take place in class, at home or in a retreat or residential situation. But the essence of training, as I am using the term, is that it concerns itself with providing for learning about learning and for improving learning proficiency. It can take place unconsciously, but a degree of purpose or organisation needs to be present if we are to distinguish it from random activity, to communicate about it, and to perfect its processes and procedures.

UNIT 6, TASK 1.2

ALISTAIR: Phew! I'm glad that lecture's over!

MARION: Yes, I know what you mean. I don't think I got much out of it at all.

ALISTAIR: I find I just can't keep up. As soon as he starts talking, I begin taking notes, but he keeps on talking, so I don't hear the bit he's saying while I'm writing about what he said before – if you follow me!

MARION: Oh yes, I know exactly what you mean. Another problem I have is keeping my mind on what he's saying. No matter how hard I try, I start thinking of something else after a while.

ALISTAIR: That's one of my problems too! Another thing is, I often get so far into a lecture, and everything's going OK, I can follow all right, and then, suddenly, I find myself wondering how we got to to the point we're on. I don't think I'm very good at keeping track of how the ideas are connected.

MARION: You're in good company, if it's any help – it's just the same for me! But another of my problems is that even if I can get down most of the points properly, I tend to forget them later on. They just don't stick in my mind. Even by the time the next lecture comes along, they're gone.

ALISTAIR: Amazing! That's my problem too! We really do have a lot in common. On another matter, I was – well, I don't suppose you fancy going to the disco tonight . . .

MARION: The disco? How did we get to that? (*bell rings*) Oh never mind – sorry, I don't have any more time to chat right now – there's the bell for my next lecture. Bye!

ALISTAIR: OK . . . bye! (*in undertone*) Drat!

UNIT 6, TASK 2.5

. . . now, there's a saying that 'accidents will happen'. But when they happen in the workplace, the cost can be very high. It is estimated that six times as many working days are lost because of accidents as because of strikes. There is also, of course, the loss in terms of human suffering, which is probably – um – incalculable. So, in this talk, I want to look at the typical causes of industrial accidents. I hope this will help us to think about how they might be reduced.

One of the first points to make is that, by and large, accidents at work are not due to workers being careless. You see, even when an accident investigation shows that a worker did not do everything he or she might have done – in theory, at any rate – to prevent an accident from taking place, it is possible to argue that it is unreasonable to expect workers to behave like robots, to always be 100% fit and alert. It is much more reasonable to expect the design and practices of the workplace to take human nature into account. Workers are actually human beings, after all!

So, what, then, are the real main causes of accidents at work?

First, there is the way machinery is designed. Too often not enough thought is given to the safety side of the design. It's all too possible to run machines without the guards and other safety devices in place. Pressure to work quicker will often lead to workers doing this. Sooner or later a mistake is made and an accident occurs.

Another major factor is the design of the workplace. The design tends to be for producing a product or a service. More often than not, it's not designed with safety in mind. You also find that some workplaces that were originally designed for one kind of process or industry will be used later on for a completely different kind of production. That naturally creates all sorts of possible dangers.

Then there's the problem of unsafe systems of working. Suppose an electrician is repairing a machine. Someone comes along, doesn't see the electrician, and switches the current back on. The equipment is now 'live' but the poor electrician is very probably dead! Even a system of notices to inform others that repair work is under way may not do the job. That's because signs get knocked off, or people may not notice them because they're tired or day-dreaming.

Let me come to a fourth main cause of these accidents. This is lack of training. Most training involves learning how to get the job done, not learning how to get it done safely. The result is that workers often learn the quickest way to do a job, but not necessarily the safest.

There's also the problem of inadequate supervision. A supervisor may not do her job properly because she doesn't know enough about the dangers. This can easily happen in industries that use complicated technology, like chemicals. Or a supervisor may simply turn a blind eye to unsafe working practices, in order to get the job done more quickly. If an accident occurs, it's the worker who will get the blame – the supervisor can claim she didn't know what was going on.

Next, number five – or is it six? – Yes, sorry, six – right, this is the danger caused by the environment – what sort of condition the workplace is in. A good example is noise. This not only damages hearing but can also cause more accidents because it puts people under stress and because it makes it difficult for you to hear warning shouts or other important noises.

Finally, some kinds of payment schemes make accidents more likely to happen. Take payment by results – PBR – for example. The reason for having a scheme like this is to get workers to work faster. The more goods or services they produce in a given amount of time, the more they are paid. But the result is often that workers under this system tend to cut down on safety if they can get the job done quicker that way. In fact, some studies have shown that there is a direct connection between an increase in productivity and the rate of accidents!

So, what can we do to minimise these problems? Well, for a start, we could . . . *(fade out)*

UNIT 6, TASK 3.4

In this talk, I'd like to give you a few basic facts and figures about the British educational system at the current time. First, some statistics, just to give you an idea of the size of the picture. Education takes about 14% of UK public spending in all – in terms of money, that comes to about £25,000 million a year. Children are required to go to school from five to sixteen years of age, and in the state sector, there are around nine million children attending about 35,400 schools. Then there are a further 580,000 pupils at independent schools – there are about 2,500 such schools, that is about 7% of the total. I should point out that these schools are known as 'public' schools, even though they are private – there is a reason for this confusing state of affairs, but please don't ask me about it at the moment!

As far as the higher or further education part of the system is concerned, the basic picture is like this. Until recently, there were 47 universities and 30 polytechnics. However, since 1992, the polytechnics have also become universities. So now there are 77 universities instead! People usually refer to the old polytechnics as the 'new' universities. Anyway, there are about 500,000 university students, and another 150,000 or so doing advanced courses at other institutions, such as colleges of higher or further education. According to government figures, 'one-third of young people receive some form of post-school education'. However, a more realistic way of putting it might be to say that only one in seven out of the eighteen- to nineteen-year-old age group enters full-time higher education – a much lower figure than in countries such as Germany, Japan and the USA. The vast majority of the post-school education in Britain, in other words, is not full-time higher education.

Let's now look more closely at some of the main features of each of the two main parts of the system – the primary/secondary and the tertiary or higher – starting with the primary/secondary level.

First of all then, how is the system run at the primary and secondary level? Well, this is obviously a complex matter, and I can't go into all the details in this talk. But two of the most important features are the National Curriculum and the examination system. The National Curriculum (which was introduced towards the end of the 1980s) says how many hours there should be each week of what subjects, in primary and secondary schools. It also says what level pupils are supposed to reach by the time they are seven, eleven, thirteen and sixteen.

As far as examinations go, there are two main ones – the GCSE and A Levels. The GCSE is taken after five years in secondary school, and is the basic qualification for going into certain kinds of jobs or for going on further in the education system. The other main exam, A Levels (the A stands for advanced) is taken after two more years of study at school, and is basically the examination you need to take in order to qualify for entrance to higher education.

Next, a word or two about matters such as class size at the primary and secondary level, and the all-important question of teachers' salaries. There is more than one figure on the subject of class size, but the general consensus seems to be in the region of one teacher to every 22 pupils. You have to remember, however, that this includes staff who may not teach a full load, such as head teachers and so on, so, in practice, it is more realistic to talk about actual numbers per class being something like 30 on average.

Pay – how much are teachers in primary and secondary schools paid? At present, there is an eleven-point basic salary scale, starting at around £11,000 a year and going up to about £18,000. That's for the ordinary classroom teacher – there are higher rates for staff with extra responsibilities, such as heads of departments, head teachers and so on. There are increasing complaints from graduates and others that these rates of pay are not high enough to compensate for the work involved. Whether that is the case or not, I leave for you to judge.

Now to move on to saying a little more about . . . (*fade out*)

UNIT 6, TASK 4.2

In today's lecture, I want to talk about the problems of stress at work. I'm going to look first of all at some of the reasons why stress occurs at work, and then we'll also spend some time thinking about what companies can do to solve this problem.

First, then, why does stress occur at work? Well, one of the most popular explanations is that it occurs because there is a mismatch between the demands placed on a person by the job and the person's ability to cope with the demands. This kind of mismatch often happens, for example, when someone is promoted because they were good at the job they did before they were promoted. Unfortunately, this does not always mean that the employee has the skills for the new, more demanding job that he or she has been promoted to. This phenomenon is often referred to as the 'Peter Principle'. In other words, people get promoted beyond their level of competence, and not being able to cope with the job is the reason they suffer stress.

There is undoubtedly some truth in the idea that stress at work is caused by the job requiring a higher level of competence than the employee has. However, this theory fails to explain the whole story. For example, it does not explain why highly competent and successful people, whose capabilities exceed the demands placed on them, can become distressed by work problems. It also fails to explain why, once a work problem has been 'solved', some employees continue to be psychologically disturbed. We have to look further than the first theory, therefore – the one about not being able to do the job – in order to find a satisfactory explanation for the cause of stress at work.

To understand why people who are good at their jobs may nevertheless suffer stress, we have to identify how people see their problems. One very revealing way of doing this is to uncover the private dialogues they engage in as they attempt to cope with the problems. These self-conversations often consist of statements such as, 'Nobody should be required to work under these conditions', or, 'If I don't complete this job on time, I'll be seen as second-rate', or 'I must maintain the highest standards all the time'.

People's dialogues with themselves reflect their ways of thinking about and interpreting the world, and thus also influence the way they behave. If such aspects of thinking are dysfunctional, in the sense that they do not help to 'solve' the problems and maintain healthy mental and emotional states, then people will become distressed.

In fact, dysfunctional ways of thinking about themselves and their work problems appear to distress people more than a lack of technical competence. This is why techniques such as 'time management' and 'objective setting' are of such limited use in helping distressed employees.

In short, stress at work may be caused not only by the employee not being capable of doing the job, but also by negative feelings about unsatisfactory conditions of service or self-induced pressures about what constitutes a satisfactory level of performance.

So, having uncovered some of the various reasons for stress at work, let us turn next to what can be done to minimise it.

One answer is for companies to invest in the mental health of employees. A comprehensive health assessment procedure, which assesses psychological as well as physical health, can identify employees suffering from stress and provide a channel for referral and counselling.

Another solution is to make sure that the right criteria are considered when matching people with jobs, especially when this involves a promotion. Instead of focusing mainly or solely on the candidate's present level of performance, it is just as or even more important to consider whether they have the potential to perform adequately in the new job. Techniques such as job trialling have a role to play here.

Finally, companies should reconsider the way they articulate their key values. Nowadays, these tend to consist of concepts such as 'achievement', 'competitiveness', 'excellence', 'competence', 'success' and the like. Unfortunately, these values are often articulated in an all-or-none manner. Indeed, anything different is seen as being second-rate.

Now, employees who attempt to put absolute views of this kind into practice make themselves immensely vulnerable to stress, since the targets they set themselves are frequently unattainable. However, if companies (and employees) learned to articulate their goals more pragmatically – in other words, in terms of what it is realistic for each employee to achieve – they would probably still achieve their targets, but without many of the costs incurred through stress.

UNIT 6, TASK 4.3B

My topic today is war crimes, and the various measures that exist to limit them, and, when they do occur, the steps that can be taken to punish the offenders, especially via war crimes trials. You have already had some background factual information on this topic, so you know that the idea of bringing war criminals to trial 'came of age' with the war crimes trials held in Germany and Japan at the end of the Second World War. Today, I want to move on from what you have read to look at how effective and just the present system for monitoring criminal behaviour in warfare is.

According to Jon Mendelsohn of the Holocaust Educational Trust, 'The Nuremberg trials were a landmark because the right to try war criminals became part of international law. They also stated that during a conflict certain standards must be maintained.'

However, both the Nuremberg trials and the ones in Japan have been criticised. It is a fundamental legal principle that an individual should not be charged for an offence which did not exist at the time the act was committed. The trials' critics have argued that this principle was violated. They say that no comparable proceedings were instituted against those who won the war.

Another important mechanism for attempting to regulate criminal behaviour in war is the 'Geneva Conventions'. In August 1949, more than 125 countries signed four Geneva Conventions for the protection of war victims and the outlawing of war crimes. The Geneva Convention also contained the principle of 'grave breaches'. These are particularly repulsive violations of the law of war, such as mistreatment of civilians or prisoners of war, torture, rape, etc. Any state which apprehends an individual who has engaged in a grave breach must either try him or her, or surrender the offender to the state where the offence took place.

Virtually all the states of the world are now party to the Geneva Conventions. Still, this fact has not led to a suppression of violence in the world. Since 1949, there have been some 200 instances of armed conflict. Most of these conflicts have not been between countries, but have occurred within the borders of one country – but only one Article in the Geneva Conventions deals with civil war. This could be because governments are unwilling to accept restraints upon their freedom of action against 'guerrillas, rebels or terrorists' who oppose them.

In 1977 an attempt was made to update the Geneva Conventions with two Additional Protocols. However, the Protocol concerning internal conflicts is still much shorter than the one updating the law of international armed conflict. In addition some states, such as the US, have rejected the Protocols which, they allege, blur the distinction between combatants and non-combatants.

Finally, let me turn to the International Committee of the Red Cross. This body watches over compliance with humanitarian law and often intervenes to help those suffering from the consequences of war.

Although the Red Cross can do little to enforce the rules of warfare, most states are eager to show that they comply with them, at least in international conflicts. The members of the international coalition which liberated Kuwait drew up guidelines for their forces to avoid violations of the law. Nevertheless, the conflict resulted in the destruction of a bunker crowded with civilians. Whatever the status of humanitarian law, war is, indeed, hell . . .

UNIT 6, TASK 5.1

JANE: Oh hello, Jill – I haven't seen you for ages. How's everything going?

JILL: Oh hi, Jane. Well, I like being here, but some things about being in a university are taking a while to get used to.

JANE: Yes, I know, it's all so different from what it was like when we were in secondary school, isn't it?

JILL: Yes, especially the lectures we have to go to and the reading we have to do.

JANE: Oh yes. I used to think we had a lot to read and take in from our teachers, but it was nothing like this – sometimes I just don't know what to do with it all.

JILL: I agree – I try to take down everything in the lectures and do all the readings carefully, but there's just too much of it to cope with!

JANE: Yes, even if I do manage to get through it all, it doesn't seem to be enough when you just tell it back in the essay.

JILL: Oh, I know what you mean – I've found that too. The teachers seem to want you to do something else with it, but I don't really know what it is.

JANE: Another thing is all these words! So many of them I never heard before.

JILL: It's the speed the lecturers speak at that I can't get used to.

JANE: Another thing I can't get the hang of is note-taking.

JILL: Yes, nobody taught us anything about that at school. It's how to keep them short enough that's my problem.

JANE: For me it's laying them out clearly. When I look back at them, I just can't make sense of them – everything seems jumbled up.

JILL: Well, it's been nice chatting to you, but I must be off – I've still got loads to read for my next Politics essay.

JANE: Yes, and I'm way behind going over my Statistics notes.

JILL: See you, then. Bye!

JANE: See you! Bye!

UNIT 7, TASK 1.1

I've been finding out how some of us prepare for our seminars. I just asked my friends what they usually did. Here's what they told me:

First of all, Jill. She said, 'I don't usually prepare beforehand because I don't have time. I find that I learn enough from the tutor and other students anyway, and it means I don't need to read everything.'

Second is Peter. He said, 'For me it's very important to be clear beforehand about the topic of the discussion – what it's really about.'

When I talked to Henry, this was his answer: 'I work out my own point of view about the discussion topic by first of all listing all the arguments for and against it.'

Next, Sally. She said, 'I spend some time thinking about recent discussions I've been involved in – what went well, what went wrong. I try to learn from these experiences.'

I asked James next. He said, 'I like to make sure I understand what we are going to talk about, so I read the materials for the discussion thoroughly beforehand.'

Wendy was the next person I asked. She said, 'I usually can't participate well in discussions, so I spend a lot of time beforehand worrying about how to avoid being asked to say much.'

The next person was – um – Andrew. He said, 'I like to talk about the topic with another student before the class so I can clarify what I am trying to say.'

Metta was the next person I spoke to. She said, 'I find it helps to think about how the others might try to counter my views about the discussion topic, and how I might deal with those objections.'

Next, Jane. She said, 'I make sure I know the exact meaning of any key words that are likely to be used in the discussion.'

Robert was next. He said, 'I try to take into account what I think the tutor's view is about the discussion topic.'

Jeffrey. He said, 'I try to think about the way the discussion is usually handled – what roles we are expected to play, what the main stages are, and so on.'

Last but not least, here's what Terry says he does: 'As I do the reading for the topic, I make notes about points I don't understand, or which I don't think are sound, or that I think need further discussion.'

UNIT 7, TASK 2.1

This is Anne's view:

'Basically, my view is that robots are likely to create more, not fewer, jobs in the future. This is because if you start using robots to produce goods, although you might have to lose some jobs at first – the ones taken by the robots – the goods you produce are likely to be cheaper and better quality than if they were produced by human beings. The result of that will be that there will be an increased demand for the goods. This will mean expanding existing factories or setting up new ones and equipping them to meet the demand. All of this will create new jobs, of course. But the biggest expansion in jobs is likely to come as a result of the extra demand for services and other goods created by the cheaper and better goods the robots produce. For example, if you produce more competitive cars as a result of using robots, more of them will be sold, and so you will have an increase in demand for the services needed to keep cars functioning – repairs, petrol, spare parts and so on. Also people will get out and about in cars more, so the leisure industry will probably expand, and so on. All this will create more jobs. So, in a nutshell, my point is that although you will lose the jobs that the robots take over, the higher standard of goods that the robots will produce will create a lot more jobs in the long run.'

Now listen to Paul's view:

'I think that robots should be resisted at all costs. If robots start to take over more and more jobs in factories, there will be mass unemployment. They have a very dehumanising effect. A lot of the pleasure you get from the work place comes from the company of other human beings. Imagine trying to discuss football or gardening with a robot! Ugh! The very thought of it makes me feel ill. And then how do you control them? I remember reading a novel by Asimov where the robots got clever enough to out-think the humans, and they took the whole country over. You see the same kind of thing in films like *2001*. Maybe they would make some goods like cars cheaper. But what value would that have? Who wants even more cars on the roads, ruining the environment? But the main problem, as I've been saying, is unemployment. Just what are you going to do with all the people the robots throw out of work? And it won't just be blue-collar workers that lose their jobs this way. You'll also get people like bank clerks, petrol station attendants, train drivers and so on being taken over by robots. And what about trade unions? They are a very important way of ensuring workers' rights are respected. But if you let robots in everywhere, you soon won't have enough workers to make the trade unions viable any longer, and that will make it even easier for the robots to take over everything. So that's my view!'

UNIT 7, TASK 2.2

MARION: I'm all in favour of it. After all, the skills needed for doing the job are very mechanical – quite within the grasp of your average robot. In fact, they already use automatic trains – more or less the same thing – at airports in places like Seattle and at Gatwick in London. This would be my view on this issue in general, in fact – in other words, if a job is simple enough to be done by a robot, then it should be. It degrades humans to waste their talents doing it.

JOHN: I would agree with you up to a point, but I think there's more to the matter than that. So, when you say we should use robots if we can for jobs where humans are really just being used as machines, then I would agree. But where I differ is about the skills involved in this particular job. I think there's a lot more to it than just getting the train from one station to another. Suppose there's an emergency of some kind. How would a robot be able to explain to the passengers what's going on and try to calm them down?

MARTIN: I think both of you are looking at the matter much too narrowly. You are both assuming that it's desirable in principle to replace humans with robots whenever you can. All you disagree about is whether robots can do all that the job involves in this particular case. I think it's also vital to consider whether it's actually right to replace humans by robots even if it is possible to do so. In other words, it may be feasible, but is it desirable?

UNIT 7, TASK 3.1

OMAR: Basically, my view is that if you don't have censorship in a state, you will have something worse.

ISABEL: What exactly do you mean by 'something worse'?

OMAR: Well, although you might say that with censorship you've got the government restricting the rights of the ordinary citizen, without censorship you could have some other force, outside the government, attempting to do that.

ISABEL: So you're saying that having censorship is more democratic than having complete freedom?

OMAR: Well, I wouldn't put it quite like that. It depends what you mean by democratic. If you mean democracy in the ideal sense of everyone being able to do whatever they like, then, OK, I would say that you can't have that and have censorship. But I think true democracy doesn't exist. That kind of democracy is really just anarchy.

ISABEL: So, just to make sure I've got this right, your point is that real democracy – as it might exist in the real world – works better if you have censorship.

OMAR: Yes, that's right.

ISABEL: OK. But can I just check a couple of things that still aren't clear to me – you said that without censorship, there might be some other force that would be free to act against the interests of the ordinary citizen?

OMAR: Right, yes, I mean, for example, that unless you ban, let's say, pornography, you allow some people in a society to exploit some of the others, and there's nothing they can do about it. Pornography is against the rights of women, so it shouldn't be allowed, it should be censored. Or take propaganda from the government in another country. If those sort of lies are allowed into your own country, it will make people turn against their own government just so that the foreign government can come and take over.

ISABEL: All right, I get the idea. But I think there's more to it than that. You're assuming that governments will always act in the best interests of their citizens.

OMAR: Yes, in my country this is always so.

ISABEL: That may well be so, but does it mean that will be the case in all the countries of the world? Isn't censorship a two-edged sword? Isn't it possible that censorship can be used to restrict the rights of ordinary citizens, not just protect them in the way you've been describing?

OMAR: Well, I'm not sure exactly what you mean. Please give me an example of the sort of problem you're thinking of.

ISABEL: Fine. Let's take a country where a dictator gets into power. Maybe the dictator is in fact a necessary evil at the time – maybe, for various reasons, the country needed a very strong leader to sort out its problems. But what often happens in such a situation is that the dictator continues to hang on to power long after he should – when the country would in fact become far stronger if it became more democratic. Some of the citizens realise that this is the case, and start to speak out. They write in the newspaper, talk on the radio and TV. So what does the dictator do? He censors them. And what is the result? Less democracy, not more.

UNIT 7, TASK 3.3

JOACHIM:
I'd like to begin by looking at some views about the causes of poverty. Some would argue that it's all the fault of the individual – whether you are poor or not, in other words, depends on you. It's your life and it's up to you to make of it what you can. If you don't take the opportunities that come along to work hard and better yourself, then that's just tough luck! It's your own fault if you don't. Now, as I said, that's one view.

Then there's another view which is basically the opposite. This view sees poverty as a result of circumstances beyond the individual's control. How can someone born into the slums of, for example, Rio de Janeiro or Calcutta, better themselves significantly? Where are the opportunities in the first place for such a person to make use of? The whole environment is so deprived that even if you wanted to, try as you may, you just can't find a way out. That's the other view, then. In other words, poverty is caused not by the individual, but the environment that individual exists in.

Now, what I'm saying is that a more satisfactory explanation is to say that there's probably an element of truth in both of these ideas. So poverty is probably caused by a mixture of factors, rather than any single one on its own. And the factors are to do with individual people, with the environment they live in, but probably also a range of other matters, such as government policy, international relations, and so on, which we haven't begun to talk about yet.

UNIT 7, TASK 4.1

ZEINAB: Well, what did you think of that?

JOHN: Well, frankly, I was rather glad when it finished!

ZEINAB: Yes, awful wasn't it? We seemed to be going round and round in circles all the time. I thought we were going to look at all sorts of different ideas about education, but we seemed to spend most of the time just talking about the first one – the one that Heinrich put forward.

JOHN: Yes, I liked his idea, but we never seemed to go on to anybody else's points. I wanted to mention a completely different view that I have, but I never got a chance.

ZEINAB: And the trouble was, the longer it went on, the more complicated it got. Half the time we seemed to be talking at cross-purposes. I'm not sure the people who were disagreeing with each other had really bothered to take the time to understand the other's point of view properly first.

JOHN: Yes, people were allowed to use all sorts of terms without saying what they meant by them. I'd never heard of half of them.

ZEINAB: Nor I. And something else that wasn't right was the way the tutor kept breaking in. He kept on jumping in with his own views.

JOHN: Yes, and he didn't seem to notice that some of us talked for ages, going on and on about the same point, taking far more than our fair share of the time –

ZEINAB: And the irony is that some other people, on the other hand, hardly opened their mouths at all! He didn't seem to mind that either.

JOHN: And I don't know what you think, but I thought some people were really rude.

ZEINAB: What do you mean exactly?

JOHN: Well, the way that François said that you can't expect the same standards of education in Africa as in Europe. I think that should have been challenged – it sounds racist to me.

ZEINAB: Oh yes, now I see what you mean. I felt the same way when Nemo was saying that women from his country shouldn't be allowed to study overseas, because they couldn't look after themselves on their own. I thought that was really sexist, but I didn't say anything because the tutor seemed to think it was OK.

JOHN: Yes, I think it was mostly his fault. He was supposed to be helping the rest of us get the most out of the discussion, but he didn't seem to be aware of that at all.

ZEINAB: One of us could have done a better job, I think!

JOHN: I agree. Why don't we suggest that to him for next time?

UNIT 8, TASK 1.3

ROSINDA: Hello, Fatu – how's everything? You look a bit down in the dumps!

FATU: Oh, hi, Rosinda. Yes, well, it's these essays we keep having to do. I must say they are getting me down a bit.

ROSINDA: Why? What's the problem with them?

FATU: Well, I find them so boring. I really don't get much out of them. They just seem to be there as a way of getting through the course. I don't really know why we have to do them – except to satisfy the teacher, of course! They just want to know if you know what they've taught you.

ROSINDA: Oh, I don't agree at all. I find them fun. I know there are some parts of them where you just have to show you've learned the subject matter, but I see most of it as a chance to express my own ideas, to show what I think. I really enjoy doing that!

FATU: Hm – well, another problem I have is I don't feel confident enough when I'm writing – I'm not sure enough I know what I'm doing. I don't feel I can improve my writing much, no matter what I do. I think it's just the way I am: I really think some people just have the knack of writing well, and there are others like me that don't.

ROSINDA: Oh, I really don't think you should feel like that at all. I feel pretty sure about what I'm doing when I'm writing, but that's not because I think I was just born that way. In fact, my writing used to be much poorer. But I decided it was just like most other things in life – something you can learn by practising and paying attention to feedback.

FATU: Well, OK, but another thing that makes me find writing very difficult is because English is not my language. I think writing in a foreign language means I will never do as well as British or American students, because they know English so well.

ROSINDA: Well, English isn't my language either, but I don't think that's really a problem. Have you ever talked to any of the British or American students about it? You should, because when I have, they've told me that they find they've got a lot to learn about essay writing as well. They don't always get high marks at all, even though they don't have so many problems with their English. So I don't see our English as being much of a problem at all.

FATU: Hm – well, that's interesting. You've cheered me up a bit – thanks!

ROSINDA: You're welcome. See you!

FATU: Bye!

UNIT 9, TASK 4.2

PROF. THOM: Oh hello, Harry! How's everything?

PROF. WHITE: Not so good, I'm afraid. I'm having an awful time with the first year's essays.

PROF. THOM: Oh dear. What's wrong with them?

PROF. WHITE: Well, first of all, some of them are very difficult to read – their handwriting is just not clear enough! Then a lot of them don't bother to leave wide enough margins down both sides of the page, and they forget to double-space, so there's no room for me to write comments.

PROF. THOM: Oh yes, I know the sort of thing you mean only too well. Another problem I find is that a lot of them still don't use headings to show what the main sections are, so you don't know where you are half the time. And they don't seem to know about putting less important information like long sets of figures and so on in an appendix, at the back, so you waste your time reading through lots of details in the main part of the essay. The result is you lose track of the main point.

PROF. WHITE: They often don't bother to put diagrams in properly either. They forget to number them or give them titles, so you don't know what the diagram is about, and it's difficult to find where they've written about it.

PROF. THOM: Something else they don't do properly is footnotes. They don't seem to realise they're just for small, extra points. Sometimes there's more in their footnotes than in the rest of the essay! It makes it very difficult to follow the main idea.

PROF. WHITE: Another thing is the information they put on the cover – actually I should say *lack* of information! You're lucky if it's got their name and the course. They don't seem to think the title is very important, or the date, and who they're doing it for. They must find it difficult to keep track of things when they're revising. I know I find it difficult keeping them sorted out in my office!

PROF. THOM: Yes. You know, I think we ought to give them more guidance at the beginning of the year about these things.

PROF. WHITE: Yes, a handout with some basic rules. Well, who's going to do it?

PROF. THOM: Well, I think they should. We can tell them what the problems are, and then they can write about how to avoid them.

PROF. WHITE: Good idea!

UNIT 10, TASK 1.1

JEFFREY: Have you ever had to do empirical research before?

KATE: Once. Have you?

JEFFREY: Yes, but only for secondary school.

KATE: What did you do it on?

JEFFREY: I was looking at how far people travelled to different kinds of shops. I used a questionnaire and interviewed shoppers.

KATE: How did it go?

JEFFREY: Not bad, but I did cheat a bit.

KATE: Oh, really!

JEFFREY: Yes, I didn't use any system of choosing who I interviewed. I just asked those who looked friendly and nice, and who I thought would answer my questions. I didn't ask many men or those shoppers who looked busy either.

KATE: That doesn't sound so terrible!

JEFFREY: Well it did probably bias the results, and I'm sure that if my teacher had known, I'd have had to do it again. I did lose marks in any case because I interviewed at small shops after school and the shopping centre on Saturday morning. What kind of research did you do?

KATE: I volunteered to do a survey for a town conservation group last summer. I was asked to investigate the kinds of shops in the local town centre. They were concerned that a lot of shops had closed, and that those that remained didn't cater to local needs.

JEFFREY: That sounds interesting. Did you have any problems?

KATE: Yes, the first few days I tried recording a list of all the properties in the town centre, because I thought that that was what they wanted. But they were only interested in past and present shops. Cafés, pubs, clubs, and so on weren't considered shops.

JEFFREY: I would have made the same mistake, I'm sure!

KATE: Once I got all the information collected, my main trouble was deciding how to present it. I ended up writing a very short report, making a map to indicate various kinds of shops, and drawing several bar graphs to indicate the number of vacant shops.

JEFFREY: Let's hope this project for Economics will go smoothly . . . (*fade out*)

UNIT 10, TASK 2.5

PETER: Hello. I'm doing a survey. Can I ask you a few questions?

MAN A: Yes. Go ahead.

PETER: How many hours do you watch TV on Saturdays?

MAN A: Um, I sometimes watch a movie in the afternoon, and if I don't go out, I watch it from eight till midnight.

PETER: What is your favourite Saturday programme?

MAN A: Not the news! A good movie, I guess.

PETER: How could Saturday viewing be improved?

MAN A: Take all the sports off television, and put on more movies.

PETER: Thank you . . . Hello. I'm doing a survey. Can I ask you a few questions?

WOMAN A: Yes.

PETER: How many hours do you watch TV on Saturdays?

WOMAN A: Usually three hours in the afternoon.

PETER: What is your favourite Saturday programme?

WOMAN A: Sports – rugby is my favourite sport.

PETER: How could Saturday viewing be improved?

WOMAN A: Put on more sports, perhaps in the early evening.

PETER: Thank you . . . Hello. I'm doing a survey. Can I ask you a few questions?

WOMAN B: OK.

PETER: How many hours do you watch TV on Saturday?

WOMAN B: It varies a lot. I suppose two or three hours.

PETER: What is your favourite Saturday programme?

WOMAN B: I don't have one. I watch whatever is on, except the soaps of course. I can't stand them.

PETER: How do you think Saturday viewing could be improved?

WOMAN B: Perhaps more quiz shows. I haven't really thought about it.

PETER: Thank you . . . Hello. I'm doing a survey. Can I ask you a few questions?

MAN B: All right.

PETER: How many hours do you watch TV on Saturdays?

MAN B: Let me see. I think about seven hours most Saturdays.

PETER: What is your favourite Saturday programme?

MAN B: *Murder By the Hour.*

PETER: How do you think Saturday viewing could be improved?

MAN B: Perhaps less news and sport and a few more horror shows . . .

PETER: Thank you . . . Hello. I'm doing a survey. Can I ask you a few questions?

WOMAN C: Go ahead.

PETER: How many hours do you watch TV on Saturdays?

WOMAN C: I don't. I work all day and go out in the evening.

PETER: Thank you . . . Hello. I'm doing a survey. Can . . . (*fade out*)

UNIT 11, TASK 1.3

CECILLE: How do you think you did, Ian?

IAN: I'm not sure. I was very rushed at the end, and didn't have time to finish the last question. I just quickly jotted down some points.

CECILLE: Didn't you outline your answers before you began?

IAN: No, that would have taken too much time.

CECILLE: But if you had done that, you wouldn't have needed to rush at the end, because you could have handed in the outline, and would have got some marks for that.

IAN: Yes . . . now that I think about it, I see what you mean. Oh, well, never mind . . . how did you do?

CECILLE: Well, I think I wrote too much. I just got carried away, and I seemed to write everything I knew about the topic. I'm not sure it was all logically connected.

IAN: Well, at least you finished.

CECILLE: Yes, that's true. I'm really glad I took the time at the beginning to read all the questions and think about them before I began. I thought at first that the first question looked easy, but then I suddenly realised it wasn't asking about just what happened in 1918 – it really wanted you to write about what the influence of 1918 was on the next ten years!

IAN: I answered that question last. But at least I had time to make my general opinion clear and put down some of my reasons for it. What helped was I think we did that question in class a couple of weeks ago, if I'm remembering correctly.

CECILLE: Look – I'm sure we both did fine! Let's go and get a coffee.

IAN: Good idea!

UNIT 11, TASK 2.3

(Telephone conversation: loud music in background when Robert speaks)

Sound of phone ringing

ARTHUR: Arthur speaking.

ROBERT: Hi, it's Robert. How's it going? Are you ready for the maths exam tomorrow?

ARTHUR: Just about. But I think I'm going to pack it in for the night now. How about you?

ROBERT: That's why I called. I thought you'd be prepared, and so maybe you could help me. I'm quite worried. I talked to Joseph and Aeshah earlier, and they're sure that we're going to be asked to derive the calculus formulae. I think I know how to use them, but we weren't taught the derivation. Do we have to know them?

ARTHUR: I wish I knew, but I'm afraid I'm not sure myself one way or the other. Just get a good night's sleep and don't worry. That's what I'm (yawning) going to do.

ROBERT: But can you tell me how to derive them, just in case? I can't find it in the book and my notes are impossible.

ARTHUR: Look, I'd like to help but the formulae for that are long and complicated. But you can look at my notes in the morning if you want.

ROBERT: I suppose that will do. I think I'll skip the sleep; I still have a lot of practice to do. Jake reminded me that we have to know our trigonometry applications and we haven't looked at those for months! Mai thinks the exam might cover last year's geometry as well. Did you hear anything?

ARTHUR: Well, I try not to listen to what other students say is or isn't going to come up. Mr Davidson said it would only cover this year's work, and would be mainly on applying the maths we've covered.

ROBERT: But surely they'll try to trick us by throwing in some things we aren't expecting. I'd like to go over everything again, but, well, you've seen where I study. I haven't kept all my notes or classwork, and the books don't seem all that clear when I go back over them. Shenaz said it was best to try and memorise the book by making up rhymes to remember the formulae. I might try that. I didn't do much work until this week. I figured that way it would be fresh in my mind.

ARTHUR: Look Robert, good luck. I have to get my sleep now. Stop worrying. See you in the morning.

ROBERT: Sleep! How can you! I think I'll make a big sandwich and get back to studying. See you, and thanks anyway. Bye.

ARTHUR: Bye.

UNIT 11, TASK 3.1

MS SMITH: George – have you had a chance to work out a marking scheme for these geography papers we're marking together yet? You said to ask you about it today.

MR JONES: Oh, yes – thanks for reminding me! Yes – well, what I was thinking of was – why don't we just assign ten marks altogether for each question? Then we can give one mark for the correct answer, two for organisation, two if the spelling and grammar are OK, two if I can read it without straining my eyes, and three if they don't waste our time with a lot of unnecessary information!

MS SMITH: Really George! You must be joking!

MR JONES: No, no, honestly I'm not. We all add and subtract marks for these things when we're tired. I have 50 essays to mark this evening, and by the time I get to the last one, well . . . you never know!

MS SMITH: Well, I have to say I really don't get the point of worrying about those sorts of things. The problem I have is that the students seem to assume that I can read their minds or that it doesn't matter whether or not they follow directions. I'm amazed the number of times students don't give their reasons for their conclusions, even when they are specifically told 'justify your answer'. That's the sort of thing I think it's most important to assess.

MR JONES: Well, that's all very well, but I still feel we have to subtract marks if the grammar, spelling, and organisation and so on aren't right. If students want to be regarded as educated, they must show they are educated.

MS SMITH: But I think the meaning of educated goes well beyond getting spelling and grammar right. I think it's the thinking, the clarity of ideas, and the creativity and development of concepts that we should be looking at – not just the grammar and spelling. And as I've been saying, I think the main problem the students have is the way they just don't appear to read and answer the questions they are actually asked . . . Well – we could talk about this all day – but I'd better get started on the marking, come what may. Look, I'll use your marking scheme this time, but next time we'll use mine – OK?

MR JONES: OK. So . . . here it is. Hope it's clear. I'd better make a beginning as well. See you!

MS SMITH: Bye.

UNIT 11, TASK 4.1

MUSA: Excuse me, Mr Jackson. Could I speak to you?

MR JACKSON: Sure. What can I do for you?

MUSA: Well, I'm a bit concerned about my score on the last exam. I thought I had done quite well. I'm not sure what I did wrong.

MR JACKSON: Right, well, I'm happy to go over the exam with you, but your score was quite good. I really wouldn't worry about it if I were you. Do you have your exam with you?

MUSA: Yes, here it is.

MR JACKSON: OK, let's see now . . . right, OK . . . now, you lost some marks because you didn't look at the underlying causes that you were asked for in question 1 . . . In question 2, you developed your main ideas quite well and gave several examples in each instance . . . In question 3, it would have been helpful if you could have looked at it from other points of view – a lot of people don't see it the way you do, you know.

MUSA: But I did mention that there were other points of view. I didn't know I needed to discuss them as well.

MR JACKSON: Like I said, you did quite well. I wouldn't worry about your mark if I were you. If you want, I'll take your paper home and write some notes for you about how you could have got higher marks.

MUSA: Thanks, I'd appreciate that. But I am still concerned about the mark. You see, I'm here on a scholarship from the government of my country, and they expect me to get high marks. In my country, 65% is hardly a pass; I expected at least 85% for what I did. I'll need an average of at least 80% to keep the scholarship.

MR JACKSON: But I never give higher than 75%, and even that is extremely rare. Your score of 65% is well above average. 70% is my usual cut-off point for outstanding work, what I believe you call an 'A'.

MUSA: Oh, I see. I didn't realise that. It's so different where I come from. If I need a statement to give to my government about your marking scheme, can you provide one?

MR JACKSON: Certainly, and I'll look at your exam again this evening. The feedback might be useful if you aren't used to our way of marking.

MUSA: Thank you. Goodbye.

MR JACKSON: Thank you for coming to see me. Bye for now.

UNIT 12, TASK 2.1

I'd like to say a word next about what the possible alternatives for transportation in the 21st century are likely to be.

One thing's for sure: there will be an increasing swing away from the attempts to solve transport problems by the main methods which have been used in the second half of the twentieth century. These are seen to have failed in most cases to live up to their promise. For example, it is now generally recognised that building major roads wherever possible only makes the problem worse, instead of solving it. All that happens is that the new roads attract more traffic than was originally anticipated, and the result is another series of bottlenecks, for which even more roads have to be built, and so on.

The other favourite main 'solution' of late twentieth century transport planners has been the rapid transit system. Under this kind of scheme, a huge new network of trains and other forms of transportation has been created in many urban areas, especially in the United States. However, the costs of building such systems have been very high, and, more important, they have generally failed to attract the passengers they were intended to cater for – those who would otherwise travel by car.

Now, highway building programmes and transit system developments are obviously different from each other in terms of the kind of transportation they are concerned with. But it's also very important to notice the way in which they are basically similar. They are both 'supply management' solutions. By this I mean they both are based on the assumption that the best way to solve transportation problems is to increase the supply of transportation of one kind or another. However, there are already signs that in the future we are likely to turn instead to the management of transportation demand as a way of solving transportation problems. In other words, attention is likely to turn more and more to ways of lessening the need to travel, or to reducing demand on the system at points or periods when it is unable to cope.

Examples of transportation demand management include so-called 'non-transportation transportation' solutions, such as the development of areas where the place of work and the home are as close as possible. Another set of ideas come under the general heading of 'auto-restraint'. This basically amounts to designing ways to discourage people from using cars, by charging high prices to enter certain zones, such as city centres, or making it impossible to drive from one part of a city centre to another, and so on.

Another likely alternative to present policies that will come more into favour in the 21st century will be the search for solutions which are based on a package of different measures, rather than on one single 'grand design'. This is again something of a reaction to the main transportation solutions which have been attempted in the twentieth century, in the sense that they have been based on the belief that there could be a single, large-scale, technological 'fix'. Solutions in the future are likely to place more emphasis on co-ordinating the development of transportation planning with socio-economic planning of other kinds. For example, there is likely to be a greater awareness of the need to plan appropriate transportation systems as an integral part of new housing or industrial developments, rather than just considering the transportation alternatives after the new development has been constructed.

In other words, there will probably be a more systemic approach in the 21st century. Please note that the word systemic I am using here is not the same as systematic. Systemic means concerned with the system in things. And that's what transportation planners are more and more likely to be concerned about in the 21st century. By this I mean seeing transportation in relation to a whole host of other factors, rather than as we have tended to see it in our century, as something separate from the rest of socio-economic life.

UNIT 13, TASK 1.1

We normally think of the answer to the question 'What is a criminal?' as being a straightforward one. A criminal is a person who commits a crime, a crime being an illegal act, something against the law.

However, once we begin to think about the matter a little further, it soon turns out to be more complicated than this. How many of us can honestly put our hands on our hearts and say we have never committed a crime? For example, how many of us have never exceeded the speed limit when driving? Or never bought items that were illegal at a certain age, such as cigarettes or alcohol? Or failed to go through the red channel at customs, in order to avoid paying duty on goods we have bought? Most of us, at one point or another in our lives, have broken the law in this way. Does this then make us criminals? I don't expect you to answer that question, let me hasten to add, at least not now and not in public! My point is that most of us, I am sure, despite committing 'crimes' like these, do not think of ourselves as criminals. This, then, is my first point: in our minds, a criminal would appear to be not always the same as someone who has broken the law.

Let me give some further examples of the difficulty of really being clear about the meaning of the term 'criminal'. Let us take the question of computer hacking. This is when an unauthorised person gains entry to a computer system. This has recently become illegal in many countries. Yet before these laws came into existence, there was widespread feeling that computer hacking was a criminal kind of activity, presumably because it made people feel worried about the threat to computerised security systems used by banks, military forces, and so on. Thus, although they broke no law until recently, computer hackers have traditionally been widely regarded as criminals. This example again serves to show the problem of trying to define a criminal simply as a law-breaker.

It would seem, in other words, that our everyday concept of what is criminal is not necessarily just what is against the law. Instead, it depends on our way of viewing the world. If I am a member of the IRA, for example, I will see myself as a 'freedom fighter', one who is committed to putting right the crimes committed by others. On the other hand, the British government will refer to me as a 'terrorist', and, because my actions are from their point of view illegal, will regard me as a criminal. In other words, the definition of who or what is a criminal depends on which side of the political fence you sit on.

Another clear example of the way concepts of crime vary is in attitudes to so-called 'victimless' crime. This kind of crime typically involves stealing money from financial institutions such as banks by taking part in illegal transactions. Very often crime committed in this way is viewed quite differently from when a bank is robbed by someone who walks in with a gun and demands to be given money. The amount stolen by either method may be the same (or, often, much less in the case of the hold-up). However, crime committed by the financial expert who manages to steal the money by some kind of illegal paper transaction is often viewed by the public as victimless – that is, it is felt that nobody suffered on a personal basis, since large financial institutions are able to absorb the costs involved, and these are seen to be impersonal kinds of organisations. There also often appears to be a sneaking admiration for the ingenuity of the criminal in such cases, which also tends to affect the view most people have of such incidents as not being crimes in the normal sense of the term. On the other hand, the ordinary bank robber is usually seen as a criminal, pure and simple.

Concepts of crime vary greatly on a sexual basis as well. This has recently been highlighted by controversy over the idea of sexual harassment in the work place. This occurs when men say or do things to women at work which offend them sexually. Most men appear to regard this type of behaviour as an extension of what they see as normal relations between men and women. Most women, however, view it as a practice which, even though it may not be illegal, should be regarded as such, and therefore as criminal behaviour. Similarly, there are often sharply divided views between men and women on the subject of wife-rape. This is said to occur when a husband forces his wife to have sex with him against her will. This has only recently been recognised as a crime in the United States and England. Traditionally, men have tended to argue that marriage gives the husband the right to have sex with his wife, with or without her consent. However, many women take the view that this is no different from the criminal act of raping another woman.

It should be obvious by now that there is no easy answer to the question of who and what is a criminal. In my next lecture . . . (*fade out*)

UNIT 14, SECTION 1

Good morning everyone! My name is Dr White, and just before I go any further, I'd like to check we've got the right people in the right room. This is Course 197, that is 'Communication and the Media'. If you should be somewhere else at this time, I suggest you go there now . . . Right, welcome the rest of you to this course. I hope you'll find the work we'll be doing together will be enjoyable and rewarding.

In the first part of today's lecture, I'll be mainly concerned with telling you what the course is going to cover, what the aims are and so on. After that, we'll begin some work on the first of our main topics.

Well, first of all, as you know, the course title is Communication and the Media, but the words communication and media are used in rather different ways by different people, so I'd better start by making clear the way in which I shall be using them. Let's take communication first. This is obviously a very wide field. It can range from the babbling of a baby to the works of Shakespeare. It can cover not only human communication but communication by other animals as well, such as monkeys, whales and bees. It can also refer to machine communication – the way computers can send messages to each other, for example. It is also possible to make a distinction between verbal and non-verbal communication – in other words, between communication involving the use of a language, such as English, and communication by other means, such as pictures, musical sounds such as drumbeats, and so on.

In this course, however, I will be using the term communication simply in relation to the media. In other words, by communication I mean the messages, images, ideas and attitudes conveyed by the media: what kind of information we receive from the media. So this course is not really a study of communication itself. It is really concerned with the way in which communication in the modern world is influenced by the media.

The key question therefore is what we mean by the term media. Here again there are a large range of possibilities. Media can be divided up into spoken, written, visual, electronic, and so on. However, in this course we are less concerned with the theoretical study of what the term media can mean than with looking at the behaviour of some of the well-known types of media that affect the daily lives of all of us. So, we will be using the term media to refer to newspapers and magazines, television, radio and advertising – in other words, the main means of mass communication in the modern world today.

Now, a word about the overall aims of the course. The overall goal is to help you understand the way in which the media shape our picture of the world nowadays. I will try to show how, in many ways, the modern world is a media world – one created by the images communicated by the media. I will also try to point out what the effects of this state of affairs are, in terms of how we see the world. In other words, I will be asking the question: how adequate is the view of the world as portrayed by the media? So, the aims are really first of all to describe the situation – to look at exactly what role the media play in communication in our daily lives, and then, secondly, to evaluate critically this state of affairs.

We'll begin working towards these overall goals by first of all having a general look at the way the language used by the media affects the kinds of messages they communicate. We'll then go on to look at a particular kind of medium, that of advertising, and the kinds of messages it communicates and what we think of their effect on the way we see things. Then we'll go on like this and look at each of the other main media that I said we'd be studying. So in the third part of the course, we'll look at television, in the fourth part the press, and so on.

Now, before I go on, are there any questions so far?

UNIT 15, TASK 1.1

(*Knocking at door etc.*)

DR JONES: Oh, hello, you must be Ali.

ALI: Yes. Dr Jones?

DR JONES: Yes, do come on in. Have a seat here. Well, nice to meet you, and thank you for coming along. As you know, I'm your adviser. My main job is to be here if you need advice about any aspect of your studies.

ALI: I see.

DR JONES: That doesn't mean I expect you will have problems, but if you do, I'm here to do what I can to help.

ALI: Right. Is there anything in particular that you think I should be paying attention to right from the beginning?

DR JONES: Well, I think the main thing that most students need to remember is that in higher education they are the ones who are ultimately responsible for managing their learning. Nobody will be around all the time telling you what to do, what not to do, when to do this or that, and so on. If you're not used to taking charge of your studies like this, then it sometimes takes a bit of getting used to. But that's what it is really essential to do, more than anything else, I would say.

ALI: OK. But suppose I don't manage to do that very well, especially at first? Suppose I get behind in my work? What should I do then?

DR JONES: Well, the really essential thing is to talk to your tutors as soon as possible. In fact, you shouldn't wait until you are behind – you should get in touch with them as soon as you *think* you are going to get behind. Never let it get to the point that you are so far behind that you get so worried about going to see the tutor about it that you keep on postponing even longer. I've known several students who did that, and by the time I found out, they were so far behind it was very difficult to help them. So, as soon as you think you're likely to have difficulties meeting a deadline, get in touch with your tutor and make an arrangement to solve the problem. Notice, by the way, that I said as soon as *you* think you're going to have a problem. It's really important to remember that it's your responsibility to realise if you're having a problem. You can't expect your tutors to chase after you and keep checking up on you. That's your job, not theirs.

ALI: Right. But suppose I have other problems, like not knowing what I should read, or how to use the library?

DR JONES: Oh yes, well then you should arrange to talk to the tutor about that as well. Make sure you find out from them what the purpose of each of the readings is – which is the best one for this or that piece of information, which one they would recommend starting with, and so on. Erm, what was your second point again?

ALI: The library . . .

DR JONES: Oh yes. Well the best thing there is to ask the librarians to help you. That's part of the service. But there are also a lot of information leaflets in the library. You might find the answers to your questions in them. So, anything else you'd like to ask me about at the moment?

ALI: Er, well, yes, er if you don't mind, just one other matter. As you know, English is a foreign language for me, so I expect I'll have some problems keeping up with the reading and so on. It's more difficult when it's not your own language.

DR JONES: Well, yes, but you should remember two things. First of all, you wouldn't be here if we didn't think your English was good enough. Secondly, if you do find you need some extra help in that direction, you can get in touch with the ELT Centre here. They provide free English classes.

ALI: Free classes? That's great – I'll remember to contact them if I need to.

DR JONES: Right. Well, I think that's about it for now. Please don't hesitate to get in touch with me again if you think there's anything about your studies I can help you with, and, meanwhile, I wish you every success.

ALI: Thank you very much. Bye!

DR JONES: Bye!